A BROWNING CHRONOLOGY
ELIZABETH BARRETT AND ROBERT BROWNING

AUTHOR CHRONOLOGIES

General Editor: Norman Page, Emeritus Professor of Modern
English Literature, University of Nottingham

Published titles include

J. L. Bradley
A RUSKIN CHRONOLOGY

Gordon Campbell
A MILTON CHRONOLOGY

Martin Garrett
A BROWNING CHRONOLOGY
Elizabeth Barrett and Robert Browning

J. R. Hammond
A ROBERT LOUIS STEVENSON CHRONOLOGY

AN EDGAR ALLAN POE CHRONOLOGY

AN H. G. WELLS CHRONOLOGY

John McDermott
A HOPKINS CHRONOLOGY

Norman Page
AN EVELYN WAUGH CHRONOLOGY

Peter Preston
A D. H. LAWRENCE CHRONOLOGY

Author Chronologies
Series Standing Order ISBN 0–333–71484–9
(*outside North America only*)

You can receive future titles in this series as they are published by placing a
standing order. Please contact your bookseller or, in case of difficulty, write to us at
the address below with your name and address, the title of the series and the ISBN
quoted above.

Customer Services Department, Macmillan Distribution Ltd
Houndmills, Basingstoke, Hampshire RG21 6XS, England

A Browning Chronology
Elizabeth Barrett and
Robert Browning

Martin Garrett

First published in Great Britain 2000 by
MACMILLAN PRESS LTD
Houndmills, Basingstoke, Hampshire RG21 6XS and London
Companies and representatives throughout the world

A catalogue record for this book is available from the British Library.

ISBN 0–333–68093–6

First published in the United States of America 2000 by
ST. MARTIN'S PRESS, INC.,
Scholarly and Reference Division,
175 Fifth Avenue, New York, N.Y. 10010

ISBN 0–312–21795–1

Library of Congress Cataloging-in-Publication Data
Garrett, Martin.
A Browning chronology : Elizabeth Barrett and Robert Browning /
Martin Garrett.
p.   cm. — (Author chronologies)
Includes bibliographical references and index.
ISBN 0–312–21795–1 (cloth)
1. Browning, Elizabeth Barrett, 1806–1861—Chronology.   2. Poets,
English—19th century—Biography—Chronology.   3. Browning, Robert,
1812–1889—Chronology.   4. English poetry—19th century—Chronology.
I. Title.   II. Series.
PR4193.G37   1998
821'.8—dc21
[B]   98–24313
                                                                              CIP

This book is printed on paper suitable for recycling and made from fully managed and
sustained forest sources.

10   9   8   7   6   5   4   3   2   1
09   08   07   06   05   04   03   02   01   00

Printed and bound in Great Britain by
Antony Rowe Ltd, Chippenham, Wiltshire

Contents

General Editor's Preface

Most biographies are ill adapted to serve as works of reference – not surprisingly so, since the biographer is likely to regard his function as the devising of a continuous and readable narrative, with excursions into interpretation and speculation, rather than a bald recital of facts. There are times, however, when anyone reading for business or pleasure needs to check a point quickly or to obtain a rapid overview of part of an author's life or career; and at such moments turning over the pages of a biography can be a time-consuming and frustrating occupation. The present series of volumes aims at providing a means whereby the chronological facts of an author's life and career, rather than needing to be prised out of the narrative in which they are (if they appear at all) securely embedded, can be seen at a glance. Moreover whereas biographies are often, and quite understandably, vague over matters of fact (since it makes for tediousness to be forever enumerating details of dates and places), a chronology can be precise whenever it is possible to be precise.

Thanks to the survival, sometimes in very large quantities, of letters, diaries, notebooks and other documents, as well as to thoroughly researched biographies and bibliographies, this material now exists in abundance for many major authors. In the case of, for example, Dickens, we can often ascertain what he was doing in each month and week, and almost on each day, of his prodigiously active working life; and the student of, say, *David Copperfield* is likely to find it fascinating as well as useful to know just when Dickens was at work on each part of that novel, what other literary enterprises he was engaged in at the same time, whom he was meeting, what places he was visiting, and what were the relevant circumstances of his personal and professional life. Such a chronology is not, of course, a substitute for a biography; but its arrangement, in combination with its index, makes it a much more convenient tool for this kind of purpose; and it may be acceptable as a form of 'alternative' biography, with its own distinctive advantages as well as its obvious limitations.

Since information relating to an author's early years is usually scanty and chronologically imprecise, the opening section of some volumes in this series groups together the years of childhood and adolescence. Thereafter each year, and usually each month, is dealt with separately. Information not readily assignable to a specific month or day is given as a general note under the relevant year or month. The first entry for each month carries an indication of the day of the week, so that when necessary this can be readily calculated for other dates. Each volume also contains a bibliography of the principal sources of information. In the chronology itself, the sources of many of the more specific items, including quotations, are identified, in order that the reader who wishes to do so may consult the original contexts.

NORMAN PAGE

Introduction

Much more is known about Elizabeth Barrett's childhood and adolescence than about Robert Browning's. He destroyed much of his own juvenilia and family correspondence while he, she, and her family carefully preserved hers. And even if more of Browning's early writing had survived, the disproportion would remain; clearly he produced nothing to rival Barrett's remarkable output of letters, stories, short plays or dramatic scenes, and poems published and unpublished. Much of this material remains comparatively little known and is therefore covered in some detail in the Chronology. (For a detailed catalogue of the manuscript material see Philip Kelley and Betty A. Coley's *The Browning Collections: a Reconstruction*.)

As knowledge of Browning's doings from the early 1830s steadily increases, the advantages of chronicling both lives together become clearer. Where Barrett can still say in October 1843 (to R.H. Horne) that 'Most of my events ... have past in my *thoughts*', Browning is to be seen, as often later, more deeply engaged in the world: theatre-going, bothering Macready about his plays, dining with friends, travelling in Russia and Italy, attending functions. There are some interesting juxtapositions: in the autumn of 1836 Barrett and Browning work at the same time on pieces as different as *The Seraphim* and *Strafford;* in May 1836 Browning meets Wordsworth at a crowded theatrical supper and two days later Barrett meets him in the quiet of John Kenyon's home. And then, with the aid of some hindsight, the lives of the two poets begin to converge. Their views on Tennyson's volume of 1842 can be compared, for example. More importantly, Barrett becomes increasingly fascinated by Browning's work, increasingly aware of their common membership – in the face of the simple directness of utterance demanded by her correspondent Mary Mitford and the like – of 'riddledom'.

From January 1845 mutual contact and discussion replace mere convergence, correspondence becomes even more important as a source, and a new disproportion occurs: 1845 and 1846 fill many more pages than other years. The courtship letters, especially when set in the context of other relationships and preoccupations, reveal more about the authors than any other writing. For a time we know almost as much about what Barrett and Browning are thinking – or at least want to be thought of as thinking – as we do about what Browning is doing in the 1880s. And fortunately for students of the poetry, one of the main subjects of the continually evolving dialogue is the composition and revision of *Dramatic Lyrics and Romances*, *Luria*, and *A Soul's Tragedy*.

Once the Brownings marry and stop writing to each other, dating more often involves detective-work. But thanks especially to Barrett Browning's many letters to her sisters, Mitford, Anna Jameson, and others, it is possible to chart their movements in Italy, France, and England fairly precisely. Sometimes the writing and publication-process of poems can also be traced in some detail. This is especially true for *Aurora Leigh*, Barrett Browning's most important work in these years, and to a fair extent for Browning's *Men and Women* (although dating of the individual poems in the volume is usually less certain). At the same time visitors like Nathaniel Hawthorne and Anne Thackeray (later Ritchie) helpfully record their impressions of life at Casa Guidi and more temporary residences.

When Barrett Browning dies and Browning returns to London there is a change of emphasis; 'RB dines with ...' is in danger of becoming a monotonous refrain in the 1860s to the 1880s. His letters and the letters, diaries, and biographies of his contemporaries show him lunching, dining, going to plays, parties, concerts, weddings, funerals, the International Inventions Exhibition, the shows at the Royal Academy and the Grosvenor Gallery. In the process, he often sees such people – to name only a few of the better known – as Dickens, George Eliot, Tennyson, Carlyle, Arnold, Trollope, Gladstone, Ruskin, Leighton, Burne-Jones, Arthur Penrhyn Stanley (Dean of Westminster), and the great violinist Joseph Joachim. He meets Clara Schumann and Turgenev and the American Jewish rights campaigner Emma Lazarus and the Shah of Persia. In his later years he knows Henry James and Thomas Hardy. Famously, Browning often strikes people he dines with as sensible, insensitive, hearty, anything but poetic, and yet the composition continues apace: James's 'two Brownings' becomes a familiar perception. But there are also, especially in the 1880s, recorded moments of greater intimacy, self-doubt, or creativity in encounters with those whom he trusts – with Edmund Gosse or Katharine de Kay Bronson for instance. Occasionally he even discusses his poems, although nowhere in the sort of detail reserved for his debate with Julia Wedgwood, at the end of the 1860s, on the morbidity or otherwise of *The Ring and the Book*. (The private Browning perhaps talked most freely about his work to his sister, whose importance in his life is made unusually noticeable by the chronological approach with its frequent 'and SB' additions.) More frequently we know (particularly from his correspondence with Eliza FitzGerald) what he has been reading. (EBB and RB were both such enthusiastic, determined, and rapid readers, that my coverage of this area is both extensive and at times, of necessity, rather selective.)

Continuity with the past was not completely lost in these later years. A chronological approach shows Browning much involved in editing or arranging publication of his wife's work, showing visitors including George Eliot her books, tables and chair, trying to protect her memory from the biographers, taking an interest in the doings of her deceiver Sophie Eckley, finding his late father 'worthy of being Ba's father'. And, as has often been remarked and chronological coverage confirms, Browning's involvement in, anxiety for, and love of their child, Pen, remained a constant feature of his life in 1861–89. Browning's attitude to the women in whom gossip said he took a more than friendly interest remains much more a matter of surmise; earlier biographers' verdicts have needed to be modified since, in the mid-1980s, Virginia Surtees proved almost conclusively that Lady Ashburton proposed to Browning, not he to her.

List of Abbreviations

EBB	Elizabeth Barrett Moulton-Barrett; Elizabeth Barrett Browning
HSB	Hugh Stuart Boyd
RB	Robert Browning
SB	Sarianna Browning
MRM	Mary Russell Mitford
AT	Alfred Tennyson

Henrietta Moulton-Barrett (later Cook) is often referred to simply as Henrietta, Arabella Moulton-Barrett as Arabel, and Robert Wiedemann Barrett Browning as Pen.

Works by EBB:

AL	*Aurora Leigh*, 1857
CGW	*Casa Guidi Windows*, 1851
EM	*An Essay on Mind with Other Poems*, 1826
Glimpses	'Glimpses into My Own Life and Literary Character', 1820–1
LP	*Last Poems*, 1862
PB	*Prometheus Bound, Translated from the Greek of Aeschylus; and Miscellaneous Poems*, 1833
PBC	*Poems Before Congress*, 1860
Seraphim	*The Seraphim and Other Poems*, 1838
Sonnets	*Sonnets from the Portuguese* (in *Poems*, 1850)
1844	*Poems*, 1844
1850	*Poems*, 1850

Works by RB:

Balaustion	*Balaustion's Adventure: Including a Transcript from Euripides*, 1871
A Blot	*A Blot in the 'Scutcheon*, 1843
BP	*Bells and Pomegranates*, 1841–6

DL	*Dramatic Lyrics*, 1842
DP	*Dramatis Personae*, 1864
DRL	*Dramatic Romances and Lyrics*, 1845
Druses	*The Return of the Druses*, 1843
Ferishtah	*Ferishtah's Fancies*, 1884
Fifine	*Fifine At the Fair*, 1872
Hohenstiel	*Prince Hohenstiel-Schwangau, Saviour of Society*, 1871
Idyls (I)	*Dramatic Idyls*, Part One, 1879
Idyls (II)	*Dramatic Idyls*, Part Two, 1880
King Victor	*King Victor and King Charles*, 1842
MW	*Men and Women*, 1855
Pacchiarotto	*Pacchiarotto, and How He Worked in Distemper, With Other Poems*, 1876
Pauline	*Pauline: a Fragment of a Confession*, 1833
Pippa	*Pippa Passes*, 1841
Red Cotton	*Red Cotton Night-Cap Country; or Turf and Towers*, 1873
Ring	*The Ring and the Book*, 1868–9
Saisiaz	*La Saisiaz; The Two Poets of Croisic*, 1878
Soul	*A Soul's Tragedy*, in *Luria; and A Soul's Tragedy*, 1846
1849	*Poems*, 1849

Other abbreviations:

Correspondence	*The Brownings' Correspondence*, ed. Philip Kelley, Ronald Hudson and Scott Lewis, 13 vols so far, Winfield, Kansas, 1984–.
Forster	Margaret Forster, *Elizabeth Barrett Browning: a Biography*, London, 1988
Gridley	Roy Gridley, *The Brownings and France: a Chronicle and Commentary*, London, 1972
Karlin	Daniel Karlin, *The Courtship of Elizabeth Barrett and Robert Browning*, Oxford, 1985
Markus	Julia Markus, *Dared and Done: the Marriage of Elizabeth Barrett and Robert Browning*, London, 1995

A Browning Chronology: Elizabeth Barrett and Robert Browning

1806

March

6 (Thurs) Elizabeth Barrett Moulton-Barrett is born, the eldest child of Edward Moulton-Barrett (1785–1857) and Mary Graham-Clarke (1781–1828), at Coxhoe Hall, County Durham. Both come from families with extensive plantations in Jamaica, where Edward was born and lived until the age of seven. EBB's beloved brother Edward Moulton-Barrett ('Bro', 1807–40) is born 26 June 1807. The other siblings most important to EBB (there are twelve children altogether, eleven of whom survive infancy) are Henrietta (1809–60), born March 1809, Arabella (Arabel, 1813–68), born 4 July 1813, and George (1816–95) born 15 July 1816. The Barretts leave Coxhoe in the Autumn of 1808 and, after a period spent mainly in London and at Mickleham in Surrey, move at the end of 1809 to Hope End, near Ledbury, Herefordshire (purchased for £24 000), their home until August 1832. The original house is converted into stables and a new mansion in exotic Turkish style is constructed.

1812

May

7 (Thurs) Robert Browning is born in Southampton Street, Camberwell (then a village near London), elder child of Robert Browning (1782–1866), clerk at the Bank of England, and Sarah Anna Wiedemann

1

(1772–1849), originally from Dundee. RB told EBB (12 June 1846) that 'Since I was a child I never looked for the least or greatest thing within the compass of their means to give, but given it was, – not for liberty but it was conceded, nor confidence that it was bestowed'. His mother is devout, highly musical, and enthusiastic about plants and animals. Thomas Carlyle remembers her as 'the true type of a Scottish gentlewoman'. RB Senior, sent to work at the family plantations on St Kitts, conceived so fervent a hatred of the slave system that he supported himself in another job for a time and then returned to England. His father's fury and the offer of a clerkship at the Bank of England in 1803 deflected him from his intention of working as an artist. He remained a keen amateur artist (especially a caricaturist), reader, and bibliophile.

June

14   (Sun) RB is baptised by Rev. George Clayton at Lock Fields Chapel, later known as York Street Congregational Church. His mother, a member of this church since 1806, will be joined *c.*1820 by his formerly Church of England father.

1814

January

7   (Fri) Birth of Sarianna (Sarah Anna) Browning (1814–1903), RB's sister. During his early career she will be his amanuensis, and again his main intimate companion and adviser when they live together after 1866.

March

EBB writes 'On the Cruelty of Forcement to Man'.

April

24   (Sun) Her father gives her ten shillings in a letter addressed to 'Miss Barrett/Poet-Laureat of/ Hope-End'

in acknowledgement of 'some lines on virtue'. EBB in *Glimpses* says that this gave her the idea of celebrating the family's birthdays in verse. The first birthday ode is written for her mother on 1 May, to be followed by many similar poems for other members of the family.

June

EBB and members of her family stay with her uncle Samuel Moulton-Barrett (1787–1837) at Carlton Hall, Yorkshire, from which they visit Matlock (EBB's 'On Visiting Matlock, Derbyshire' is dated 11 (Sat). They go on to stay with her maternal grandparents John and Arabella Graham-Clarke at Fenham Hall, Newcastle upon Tyne, until September. Here EBB writes poems on first seeing the sea at Tynemouth and on hearing Angelica Catalani sing in Newcastle.

October

She writes her stories 'Sebastian or the lost Child a Tale of other Times' and 'The Way to humble Pride'.

At eight EBB is reading Greek history and poems including James Beattie's *The Minstrel* (1771–4), Pope's translation of Homer's *Iliad*, passages from *Paradise Lost* suggested by her mother, *The Tempest*, and *Othello*.

1815

Around this year EBB writes 'On putting up the clock at Hope End'.

June

18   (Sun) Battle of Waterloo.

August

EBB writes her essay 'Where can happiness be found?'

October

17   (Sun) EBB and her parents, after staying some days in London at the home of her paternal grandmother Elizabeth Moulton in Baker Street, set off for Paris

(crossing the Channel on 18). She records the journey in 'Notes on a Trip to Paris October and November 1815'. They sleep at Calais on 18 and Boulogne on 19 and look at the 'cathedral' (the church of Saint-Saulve) at Montreuil before spending the night of 20 at Hôtel de l'Europe, Abbeville. On 21 they admire the 'very handsome cathedral' at Amiens and continue through country 'full of Prussian soldiery' to Clermont. On 22 they visit Chantilly and reach Paris, where they find rooms at the Hôtel de Rivoli. They see the Louvre, Malmaison, the china, glass and carpet manufactories, the Pantheon, Notre-Dame, the Jardin des Plantes, Les Invalides, and Versailles.

November

10   (Fri) EBB's uncle Samuel Moulton-Barrett arrives in Paris. With him EBB and her parents go to the Théâtre Français to see François Joseph Talma (she is 'rather disappointed') and to the Opéra Comique where she is delighted with the ballet.

13   The Barretts leave Paris. They stay at St Germain on 13–14 and at Rouen, where they see the cathedral and the site of Joan of Arc's burning, on 15–16. Sailing from Boulogne on 16, they reach London on 17 or 18 and again stay in Baker Street (until some time in December).

1816

c. January–February

EBB begins learning French. She starts Latin by May. Her French progresses well enough for her to write, by the end of the year, the short French classical tragedy 'Régulus' for herself, Bro and Henrietta to perform; later she remembers sitting in her 'house under the sideboard' in the dining-room to 'concoct' one of the soliloquies (to RB, 15 January 1846). The unpublished fragment 'Cleone Agripine' may date from the same period.

July

16   (Tues) She dedicates to her grandmother Elizabeth Moulton her manuscript 'Julia or Virtue a novel'.

1817

Probably this year EBB reads Maria Edgeworth's *Manoeuvring* (in *Tales of a Fashionable Life*, 1809) and *Patronage* (1814). Now or soon afterwards she also reads Goethe's *Werther* and works by Paine, Hume, Voltaire, Rousseau, and Wollstonecraft.

This summer she begins to learn Greek and to write *The Battle of Marathon* (1820).

RB at about five (according to his letter to EBB of 25 August 1846) writes his first poetry. It is inspired by 'scraps' of Ossian.

September

17   (Wed) EBB and some of her siblings – probably Bro and Henrietta – perform her (now lost) 'Socrates, or the Laurel of Athens'.

About now she drafts a letter to Lord Somers, as Lord Lieutenant of Herefordshire, protesting against the suspension of the Habeas Corpus Act.

c. **November**

She reads Byron's *The Corsair* (1814).

1818

June

EBB writes her autobiographical essay 'My Own Character', expressing her strong preference for reading and writing over needlework, drawing, dancing and music.

November

In a letter to her uncle Samuel she discusses works including Madame de Sévigné's letters and Byron's *Childe Harold*, Canto Four.

1819

This year or the following RB becomes a weekly boarder at Peckham School (77 Queen's Road, Peckham), where he is taught until about the age of ten by the Misses Ready and then receives a classical education from their brother, Rev. Thomas Ready (d. 1866), up to fourteen (1826). He writes (*c.* 1820–1) a complimentary poem to Ready, which he later remembers as 'great *bosh*' and also, he will tell Alexandra Orr, 'had some of his own boyhood dramatic works put on'.

May
4   (Tues) EBB writes 'First Greek Ode … To Summer'.

c. June–July
The Barretts are at Worthing.

September
EBB and her siblings Bro, Henrietta, Samuel (1812–40) and Charles John ('Stormie', 1814–1905) present EBB's now lost 'The Tragedy of Laodice' at Hope End.
The Battle of Marathon is finished by the end of the year.

1820

March
6   (Mon) EBB's *The Battle of Marathon* is privately printed (fifty copies) on her fourteenth birthday, dedicated to her father 'whose admonitions have guided my youthful muse, even from her earliest infancy' and who pays for the printing.
10   EBB's uncle Samuel is elected MP for Richmond in Yorkshire (until 1828).

April
c. 1 (Sat) Bro, after some time at his grandmother Moulton's house, goes to school at Charterhouse, prompting EBB's 'Written in the Anguish of Bidding Farewell to My Beloved Bro'.

This summer EBB writes the first scene of a projected play –
a dialogue, set in 1817, between Princess Caroline (Queen
Caroline from January 1820) and Princess Charlotte.

In 1820–1 she writes *Glimpses*, discussing her early reading,
determined approach to literature and learning, independence of spirit, attempts at self-control, and devotion to
Bro.

1821

Probably this year EBB sends a letter to Thomas Campbell
(the poet), editor of *The New Monthly Magazine*, opposing
an 1820 article on 'Talking and Talkers' in the guise of one
renowned for forty years as a silent man. Probably her un-
titled essay on truth (*Correspondence* 1.109–12) also belongs
to this year.

February
She writes her essay 'My Character and Bro's Compared'.
She sees him as reasoning more acutely than her, less fiery,
humbler. Their separation is difficult to bear, but their love
remains undiminished.

April
EBB and her sisters are unwell. Symptoms include
headaches and muscular convulsions which, in her case,
will continue into the summer.

May
Her 'Stanzas, Excited by Some Reflections on the Present
State of Greece' is published in *The New Monthly Magazine*.

July
EBB's 'Thoughts Awakened by Contemplating a Piece of
Palm Which Grows on the Summit of the Acropolis at
Athens' is published in *The New Monthly Magazine*.
EBB who, with Henrietta, had measles in June, remains
unwell and is sent to recuperate at the Spa Hotel,
Gloucester. Several doctors are consulted but no certain

diagnosis is reached. Since she thinks her spine is swollen, Dr Coker decides to put her in a 'spine crib' which probably weakens her further. Opium (morphine), on which she will be reliant for much of her life, is also prescribed.

September
About now she writes 'Fragment of an "Essay on Woman"', arguing for the equality of women, under the influence of Mary Wollstonecraft's *A Vindication of the Rights of Woman*.

1822

c. May
She returns from Gloucester to Hope End.

August
28 (Wed) Thomas Campbell sends encouragement and 'unsparing criticism' in response to poems – 'Leila, A Tale: with other Poems' – dedicated to him by EBB. When she sends another manuscript (possibly 'The Enchantress') at the beginning of December he indicates that he has 'neither eye-sight nor leisure' to comment on further specimens of her work. In about May 1823, nevertheless, she sends him an early version of her prose piece 'A Thought on Thoughts' (see 23 July 1836).

1823

June
Probably this month, several members of the Barrett family, including EBB, take up residence in Boulogne (until January 1824) at least in part so that she can improve her French. A friend met at this time is the likely subject of 'To Victoire, on her Marriage' (PB).
During 1823–5 EBB reads a great number and variety of books, recorded in notebooks now at Wellesley College, including travel books, history, literary and theatrical

memoirs, and Locke's *An Essay Concerning Human Understanding*.

November

7   (Fri) Execution of the Spaniard Rafael del Núñez Riego, who 'lived the Patriot's life' but 'was dragged to die the traitor's death'. Probably within the next few months EBB writes 'Lines on the Portrait of the Widow of Riego' (in *EM* as 'On a Picture of Riego's Widow'), in response to which Teresa del Riego sends her a lock of hair. Following Teresa's own death in 1824 EBB will write 'The Death-Bed of Teresa del Riego' (*PB*).

1824

The Brownings move to Hanover Cottage, Southampton Street, Camberwell, their home until December 1840.
Financial worries begin for EBB's father and uncle Samuel following a decision against them, and in favour of their cousins the Goodin-Barretts, concerning slaves and property in Jamaica inherited from their grandfather Edward Barrett. Long-term consequences include Samuel's departure for Jamaica in 1827 and the sale of Hope End in 1832.

April

19   (Mon) Death of Byron (news of which reaches England in May). His work heavily influenced EBB's 'Leila' in 1822 and RB's *Incondita c.* 1826. EBB imagined becoming his page and RB would, he will tell her on 22 August 1846, have travelled miles for a sight of 'a curl of his hair or one of his gloves'.

May

28   (Fri) EBB presents her father with 'To my dearest Papa. On his birthday' (revised for *EM*).

June

30   (Wed) Her 'Stanzas on the Death of Lord Byron' (*EM*) is published in *The Globe and Traveller*.

July

She visits 8 Cambury Street, Cheltenham to stay with her grandmother and aunt Arabella Graham-Clarke (1785–1869), known in the family as 'Bummy'.

December

28 (Tues) EBB's poem for Stormie's tenth birthday will become the substance of 'Memory' in *EM*.

1825

March

5 (Sat) EBB's *An Essay on Mind* is finished by this date. By 13 December it has been in the press 'for nearly five months' and 'thro' the weekly calls on me for proof-correcting, is a constant source of annoyance'.

26 Bro sends her 'a very beautiful *silver remember* medal of Lord Byron'.

July

EBB and her sister Henrietta begin an eleven-month stay with their grandmother Moulton in Hastings.

November

19 (Sat) EBB's 'The Rose and the Zephyr' is published in *The Literary Gazette, and Journal of the Belles Lettres*.

1826

Probably this year RB writes 'The Dance of Death' and 'The First-Born of Egypt'. These appear to be all that survives of *Incondita*, the early collection of verses most of which he later destroyed. This year or in 1827 his cousin James Silverthorne gives him a copy of Shelley's *Miscellaneous Poems* (1826).

RB leaves school and continues his education at home (until 1828) with further training in music, fencing, boxing, drawing, and dancing. He studies French with Auguste Loradoux of Walworth. This seems also to be the period in which, influenced by Shelley, he is a vegetarian.

March

25   (Sat) EBB's *An Essay on Mind with Other Poems* is published by James Duncan, London (underwritten by
Mary Trepsack (1768?–1857), grandmother Moulton's
companion). The Barretts received advance copies on
27 February.

May

6   (Sat) EBB's 'Irregular Stanzas' is published in *The
Literary Gazette, and Journal of Belles Lettres.*

June

About now EBB and Henrietta return to Hope End from
Hastings. On the way they perhaps visit Tunbridge Wells
and Penshurst, subject of EBB's 'The Picture Gallery at
Penshurst' (*PB*).
Uvedale Price (1747–1829), a well known classical scholar,
sends praise and criticism of 'An Essay on Mind'.

October

EBB and Henrietta visit Uvedale Price at Foxley. EBB
starts checking and commenting on the proof sheets of
his *An Essay on the Modern Pronunciation of the Greek
and Latin Languages* (1827). He accepts many of her
suggestions.
Late this year she starts writing 'The Development of
Genius'.

1827

January

EBB's 'Who art thou of the veiled countenance' is published in *The Jewish Expositor and Friend of Israel.*

February

4   (Sun) She writes an autobiographical essay on her
father's discouraging response to her poem 'The
Development of Genius', which he considers too
inexplicit, beyond her grasp, and worthy only to be
burnt. She is 'mortified' and 'grieved' to discover that

he thinks her talents so limited. Uvedale Price is contrastingly sympathetic.

This month (as also in November 1826) EBB is at Eastnor Castle, home of Lord Somers, for several days.

March

7   (Wed) EBB's reply to a letter on *EM* from Hugh Stuart Boyd (1781–1848) initiates her correspondence with the blind scholar. She is 'solicitous to obtain' and 'earnest in valuing, a fair and candid criticism'.

26   She sends – in fact a week too early – 'To Uvedale Price Esqr. on his [eightieth] Birthday'.

November

3   (Sat) She explains, in a letter to HSB, her difficulties in coming to meet him; she has delayed as long as possible telling him that her father believes that as 'a young female' she cannot pay the first visit 'without overstepping the established observances of society'. (Forster, p. 41, casts doubt on how much her father really objected to such a meeting.)

10   Death of Arabella Graham-Clarke, EBB's maternal grandmother.

23   Sarah Flower, writing to W.J. Fox about her (later overcome) religious doubts says that 'It was in answering Robert Browning that my mind refused to bring forward argument'. RB has been encouraged as a poet by Sarah (1805–48) and Eliza Flower (1803–46) in the mid-1820s. He will know them well again after *Pauline* (1833).

24   RB learns, in response to an enquiry in *The Literary Gazette*, that he can obtain works by Shelley from the publishers Hunt and Clarke. His mother buys for him first editions of almost all the works. At about the same time he obtains Keats' *Endymion* and *Lamia* volume.

1828

February

12   (Tues) Baronetcy conferred on Uvedale Price.

March

3   (Mon) EBB talks in a letter to HSB of her preference for Homer to Virgil and argues the cause of the modern Greeks, nearing the end of their War of Independence (1821–9).

13   HSB is displeased, and EBB embarrassed, when she passes him on the road without stopping to meet him. As a result she obtains her father's permission to do as she likes with regard to visiting him. She meets him briefly on 17 after a carriage accident on the way to his house (Ruby Cottage, Malvern Wells) in which Henrietta is slightly injured.

April

16   (Wed) She eventually succeeds in calling on HSB, the first of many regular visits to talk and read Greek to him. Partly under his encouragement she reads, during the next few years, much of the Greek ancient and patristic corpus.

22   RB is enrolled by his father, at his own request, at the London University (the future University College, London), a newly established college for Dissenters and others who cannot subscribe to the Anglican Thirty-Nine Articles as required by Oxford and Cambridge. RB Senior, who was one of the original subscribers to or 'proprietors' of the university in 1825, recommends him for his 'Moral Character' and 'his unwearied application, for the last 6 years, to the Greek, Latin and French languages'.

May

The Boyds move to Woodland Lodge, Great Malvern.

July

7   (Mon) Death at Cheltenham of EBB's mother, Mary Moulton-Barrett. Although she has been ill with rheumatoid arthritis for some time, her death is unexpected. EBB will remember her (to RB, 27 August 1846) as having 'a sweet, gentle nature, which the thunder' –

her husband's difficult nature, at least from EBB's point of view at this later time – 'a little turned from its sweetness – as when it turns milk'.

Visits to HSB cease until next summer.

October

Late this month RB begins to attend lectures at the London University. After a few days in lodgings in Bedford Square he commutes from home. He studies Latin, Greek, and German.

1829

Probably this year he attends lectures on midwifery and physiology by Dr James Blundell at Guy's Hospital.

May

4   (Mon) RB Senior writes 'to communicate my son's determination to withdraw from the London University, (an event as painful as it was unexpected)'.

At around this time RB begins to study Italian language and literature with Angelo Cerutti.

June

c. 21   (Sun) EBB is at Malvern Wells with Mary Trant (cousin of her grandmother Moulton).

July

EBB's 'Wisdom Unapplied' is published in *The Gleaner*.
Either this month or next she is again at Eastnor Castle for a few days.

September

14   (Mon) Her friend Sir Uvedale Price dies. At some point between now and the end of October she writes 'To the Memory of Sir Uvedale Price, Bart.' (*PB*).

December

29   (Tues) Death of Elizabeth Moulton, who leaves her granddaughter EBB £4000.

1830

By the early 1830s RB, after a period of questioning (see 23 November 1827) or even Shelleyan atheism, has adopted more orthodox beliefs. He and SB attend both the York Street Congregational Church and Camden Chapel (Church of England).

May
EBB stays with the Boyds at Woodland Lodge, Great Malvern.

June
26 (Sat) Death of George IV; succeeded by William IV.

August
2 (Mon) HSB, on the occasion of a visit by Princess Victoria, delivers an 'Address to Malvern'. EBB sends him 'The Reply of Malvern to the address of H.S. Boyd Esqr ...'.
3 Writing to HSB after the July revolution has overthrown Charles X of France, she declares that 'the French nation is not an interesting nation, – and yet no English ear ought to like hearing its chain clanking over the sea'.

September
20 (Mon) EBB goes to stay with the Boyds at Woodland Lodge until 7 October.

October
21 (Thurs) RB sees Macready as Hamlet at Drury Lane.

1831

March
21 (Mon) First Reform Bill defeated.
23 HSB sends EBB C.G. Heyne's *Homeri Carmina* (1802).

May

18   The Boyds move from Woodland Lodge, Great Malvern, to Ruby Cottage, near Malvern Wells (also their home in 1827–8).

Between mid-May and 20 August EBB's friend Eliza Cliffe paints her portrait.

31   EBB's 'Kings' appears in *The Times*.

31   Bro is among the speakers at a celebration dinner in Ledbury for the pro-Reform MP Kedgwin Hoskins.

June

4   (Sat) EBB begins her Diary (to 23 April 1832). Here she discusses her reading, her anxiety about the possibility of leaving Hope End, her feelings of uncertainty about HSB's feelings for her, her jealousy of other young women who visit him (and even, in the case of Henrietta Mushet, read Greek to him), and her anger with herself for entertaining such feelings. She is also nervous at the prospect of HSB's leaving the area, which his wife and daughter are urging him to do.

July

12   (Tues) EBB rereads Ann Radcliffe's *The Mysteries of Udolpho* (1794). On 14–16 she reads Susan Ferrier's novel *Destiny*. Her reading this summer also includes poems by Hugo and Lamartine and works by Pindar, Aeschylus, Euripides, and Epictetus.

16 She receives *Homeri ... Opera*, ed. Friedrich Wolf (1806) from HSB.

August

8   (Mon) – 11 She reads Mary Shelley's *The Last Man* (1826).

17–19   EBB reads most of Keats' poems. She finds them somewhat disappointing having already seen the finest passages in extracts. *Hyperion*, however, contains poetry of some grandeur. On 24 she finds Shelley's *Adonais* 'perfectly exquisite' (Diary).

25 Hope End is put up for sale by auction but withdrawn when bids fail to reach the reserve price. Family tension about the possibility of leaving has been much exacerbated, since the spring, by lack of information from Mr Barrett.

September
14 (Wed) EBB is reading Mary Brunton's novel *Self-Control* (1811), where she finds interesting 'the combination of fortitude and delicacy'.

October
7 (Fri) Second Reform Bill rejected by the House of Lords.
18–20 EBB stays with the Boyds at Ruby Cottage.

November
5 (Sat) She writes her poem 'The Weakest Thing' (*Seraphim*) for possible inclusion in her friend Nelly Bordman's album.
5 EBB's brothers Bro and Sam go to Reform meetings at Hereford and Worcester.
16 She is reading Camoëns; on 17 she begins to write 'Catarina to Camoens' (see October 1843). On 30 she starts copying it into Annie Boyd's album (continuing on 13 January 1832).
8–14 EBB again stays at Ruby Cottage.
26–30 She is at Eastnor Castle.

1832

By now RB is a member of the 'Set' of friends who meet for 'colloquials' in the 1830s and, more irregularly, the early 1840s. They include Chris Dowson (1808–48), Joseph Arnould (1814–66) and Alfred Domett (1811–87).

January
9 (Mon) EBB writes her poem on recent cholera outbreaks 'The Pestilence' (published in *The Times* on 13).

February

1   (Wed) – 15 She works on her translation of Aeschylus' *Prometheus Bound*. She will soon come to feel that the speed of completion is only too apparent. (The revised version, published in *1850*, dates mainly from 1844–5).

May

The Boyds, to EBB's distress, leave Malvern.

18   (Fri) Some time between now and 29 June RB goes to a production of Beethoven's *Fidelio* at the King's Theatre.

June

Probably this month Hope End is sold.

4   (Mon) Third Reform Bill passed. ('We may be prouder of calling ourselves English than we were before it past', EBB writes to HSB on 9.)

9   EBB tells HSB that she has read de Staël's *Corinne* 'for the third time, and admired it more than ever'.

August

23   EBB and most of her family leave Hope End. They spend the night in Bath.

24   The Barretts take up residence at Rafarel House, Sidmouth, Devon. Here one of her principal acquaintances will be Rev. George Barrett Hunter, minister of the Independent Chapel until early 1835.

October

22   (Mon) RB sees Edmund Kean as Richard III at the King's Theatre, Richmond, and conceives as a result 'the childish scheme' of writing novels, operas, speeches, '&c &c' under different pseudonyms so that 'the world was never to guess' that all the artists 'were no other than one and the same individual'. *Pauline* was conceived as 'the first work of the *Poet* of the batch'. SB will later maintain that he began work on the poem before this date.

December
By 11 (Tues) HSB has, at EBB's encouragement, come to live in Sidmouth (until spring 1834).

1833

January
RB completes *Pauline* (probably).

February
1 (Fri) His father gives him a 1795 copy of Bernard de Mandeville's *Fable of the Bees* (1714), a work eventually drawn on in the 'Parleying With Bernard Mandeville' (*Parleyings*, 1887).

March
7 (Thurs)? RB's *Pauline: a Fragment of a Confession* is published, anonymously, by Saunders and Otley. Publication and advertising are paid for (£30) by his aunt, Christiana Silverthorne. (SB knows about the poem but their parents do not.) He sends twelve copies to Fox, who sends one on to J.S. Mill. No copies are sold. RB sends W.J. Fox 'Impromptu on Hearing a Sermon by the Rev. T[homas] R[eady] Pronounced "Heavy"'.

April
Fox's mainly favourable review of *Pauline* appears in *The Monthly Repository*: it is 'evidently a hasty and imperfect sketch' but 'gave us the thrill, and laid hold of us with the power' of genius.

May
11 (Sat) EBB's translation of Aeschylus' *Prometheus Bound* is published by A.J. Valpy at 5s.
25 RB attends Edmund Kean's funeral at Richmond.

August
28 (Wed) Act emancipating slaves (subject to certain transitional restrictions). EBB, whose family finances are much involved in sugar plantations, expresses mixed feelings:

'the late bill has ruined the West Indians. That is settled. The consternation here is very great. Nevertheless I am glad, and always shall be, that the negroes are – virtually – free!' (to Julia Martin, 7 September).

September
The Barretts move from Rafarel House to Belle Vue, Sidmouth.

October
30   (Wed) Fox returns to RB the copy of *Pauline* with comments by J.S. Mill.

December
18   EBB gives Mary Maddox a copy of *PB* in which – presumably now or later – she writes 'The Tears of Jesus', an early version of 'The Weeping Saviour: Hymn III' (*Seraphim*).

1834

February
6   (Thurs) RB writes 'On the deleterious effects of tea', another version of which dates from as late as June 1883.
Setting off late this month he travels to St Petersburg via Holland, Germany, and Lithuania with Chevalier George de Benkhausen, Russian consul general in Britain. 'Porphyria' and 'Johannes Agricola' (see January 1836) may have been written during this period.

June
RB arrives back in London. Soon afterwards he applies to be appointed to a diplomatic mission to Persia. On 4 February 1835 he writes to Sarah Flower Adams that 'I don't go to Persia'.
Most likely this summer he begins work on *Sordello*, which will occupy him for long periods until February 1840. (Composition will be punctuated by work on *Paracelsus* in 1834–5 and on *Strafford* between July 1836 and May 1837, and by his travels in 1838.)

August

1 (Fri) RB meets (through his uncles William and Reuben Browning) Count Amédée de Ripert-Monclar (1807– 71), a French aristocrat with literary and artistic inter- ests and possibly an agent in England for supporters of the deposed Bourbons. On 15 they are at the British Museum together and then at the Brownings' house. Between now and Monclar's departure on 17 September they see each other very frequently.

17 RB writes the sonnet 'Eyes, calm beside thee ...', pub- lished anonymously in the October *Monthly Repository*.

September

He begins work on *Paracelsus*. The subject of the poem is first suggested by Monclar, to whom it will be dedicated in 1835.

October

Monclar's review of his uncle the Marquis de Fortia d'Urban's *Essai sur l'origine de l'écriture* in *The Metropolitan Magazine*, translated by RB.

November

19 (Wed) EBB is 'in an enthusiasm about' Bulwer's *The Last Days of Pompeii* (1834). RB has read it by March 1835.

December

5 (Fri) By this date *Paracelsus* is finished in one form. Expansion and revision follow between now and, probably, February 1835.

31 RB and Monclar are listed as members in the first journal of the Institut Historique in Paris.

1835

February

RB's letter replying to an 'Essay on Debt' is included in *The Trifler*, the amateur and probably short-lived magazine of the 'Set'.

c. 10 (Tues) He sees Macready as Bertulfe in George Lovell's *The Provost of Bruges*.

March

2   (Mon) RB writes to Monclar about *Paracelsus*, which
       has been 'done in 3 or 4 months' and is 'novel, as I
       think, in conception and execution at once'. On 27 he
       tells Fox that it is 'a sort of dramatic poem made after
       rules of my own' in which he has put forth his whole
       strength.

c. 29 Between now and 15 April RB calls on the publisher
Edward Moxon, with a letter of introduction from Fox, in
hope of placing *Paracelsus* with him. He also tries John
Murray in early April.

June

The Barretts again live at Rafarel House, Sidmouth (until
December).

July

16   (Thurs) RB probably sees Maria Malibran perform at
       Drury Lane.

About now he takes a considerable share in a work by his
French teacher Auguste Loradoux and Charles Le Roy, *Le
Gil Blas de la jeunesse, à l'usage des écoles* (1835).

August

15   (Sat) *Paracelsus* is published (price 6s.) by Effingham
       Wilson, the first work to appear under RB's name.
       Publication is paid for by RB Senior.

September

EBB's 'Stanzas Addressed to Miss Landon, and Suggested
by her "Stanzas on the Death of Mrs. Hemans"' (*Seraphim*)
is published in *The New Monthly Magazine*.

6   (Sun) John Forster's favourable review of *Paracelsus* in
       The Examiner, predicting for RB 'a brilliant career, if he
       continues true to the present promise of his genius', is
       among the responses which spread his fame and give
       him entry into wider social circles (see especially 26
       May 1836). Forster also writes about RB in 'Evidences
       of a New Genius for Dramatic Poetry' in *The New
       Monthly Magazine* for March 1836.

November
RB's 'The King' is published anonymously in *The Monthly Repository*; it will be revised as the song in Part Three of *Pippa*
27   (Fri) He is introduced to W.C. Macready in the house of W.J. Fox. RB sends him a copy of *Paracelsus*.

December
c. 2   (Wed) The Barretts move to 74 Gloucester Place, London.
7–8   Macready reads *Paracelsus* and finds it daring, sometimes obscure, and evidence that RB 'can scarcely fail to be a leading spirit of his time'. On 31 Macready entertains a group including RB and Forster, who meet for the first time. Afterwards Macready notes in his diary that RB 'looks and speaks more like a youthful poet than any man I ever saw'.

1836

This year or later RB begins learning Hebrew.

January
Under the initial 'Z' he publishes, in *The Monthly Repository*, 'Porphyria' and 'Johannes Agricola' (*DL*, grouped as *Madhouse Cells*; subsequently 'Porphyria's Lover' and 'Johannes Agricola in Meditation').

February
3   (Wed) RB sees Macready as Othello.
16   Forster, Macready and RB 'talked over the plot of a tragedy which Browning had begun to think of: the subject, Narses'.

March
19   (Sat) EBB's 'Man and Nature' (*Seraphim*) appears in *The Athenaeum*.

April
RB meets Thomas Carlyle. At their first encounter the poet, in his green riding-jacket, makes a bad impression;

according to RB in 1881 if they had not met again he might have been recorded as 'a poor scribbling-man with proclivities for the turf and scamphood'. Carlyle soon begins, however, to take a great interest in him.

May

RB's 'Still ailing, wind?' is published anonymously in *The Monthly Repository*.

c. 7   (Sat) Publication of Forster's *Life of Strafford* (Lives of Eminent British Statesmen, vol. 2), in the completion of which RB took a substantial undisclosed share.

26   At supper after the first night of Thomas Noon Talfourd's tragedy *Ion* at Covent Garden Talfourd proposes a toast to RB, 'the youngest poet of England' and William Wordsworth tells him 'I am proud to drink your health, Mr Browning'. Walter Savage Landor and Mary Russell Mitford are also among those present. Afterwards Macready asks RB to write a play for him and RB suggests 'a drama on Strafford'.

27   John Kenyon, EBB's distant cousin and increasingly close friend, introduces her to Mary Russell Mitford (1787–1855). They go to the zoo and the Park Place Diorama. MRM will soon become her principal correspondent.

28   EBB meets Wordsworth and Landor at Kenyon's home. She finds Landor 'brilliant'; his 'eminent talent' contrasts with the 'great genius' of the more simple-mannered Wordsworth (to Julia Martin, 7 December).

June

8   (Wed) By now she has written 'The Sea-Mew' (*Seraphim*) in the album of Louisa Bithia Courtenay, daughter of a friend of Kenyon.

July

EBB's 'The Romaunt of Margret' (*Seraphim*) is published in *The New Monthly Magazine*.

2   (Sat) 'The Seaside Walk' (*Seraphim*) is published in *The Athenaeum*, as on 23 is her essay 'A Thought on Thoughts'.

August

10   (Wed) EBB discusses *Paracelsus* in a letter to MRM: she wishes it were more concentrated and dislikes some of the references to 'the divine Being', but feels 'palpable power! a height of & depth of thought, – & sudden repressed gushings of tenderness which suggest to us a depth beyond, in the affections'.

October

'The Poet's Vow' (*Seraphim*) is published in *The New Monthly Magazine*.

Late this month and in November EBB works on *The Seraphim*.

31   (Mon) RB has finished most of *Strafford*.

November

1   (Tues) Macready expresses his first doubts about the 'likely dramatic power' of *Strafford*. After delays partly occasioned by the fact that Act Four is not complete, on 21 Macready criticises the play 'frankly' and RB promises 'to do everything needful to the play's amendment'. Rereading the manuscript on 23, Macready worries that earlier he was 'too much carried away by the truth of character to observe the meanness of plot, and occasional obscurity'.

26   EBB's 'Your lyrics found me dull as prose ...' is included in a letter to HSB.

December

4   (Sun) She tells MRM that she has read extracts from Beaumont, Fletcher, and Ford, and knows Massinger and Jonson, whose *Sad Shepherd* and *Catiline* contradict his reputation for unpoetic pedantry.

20   RB gives Macready 'the omitted scenes in his play'. Macready feels that the play 'still is not up to the high-water mark'.

1837

Some time this year RB goes to Paris to visit his uncle, William Shergold Browning (1797–1874), who works for Rothschild's in Paris, living at 15 Rue Laffitte, between 1824 and the mid-1840s.

Perhaps early this year RB writes an epitaph ('Words we might else have been compelled to say ...') for the parents and siblings of his friend James Dow.

January
EBB's 'The Island' (Seraphim) appears in *The Monthly Magazine*.

March
18 (Sat) – 19 Macready rereads *Strafford*, about which he still has mixed feelings ('I fear [it] is too historical'). On 21 he reads through and discusses the play with RB. Reading it yet again that evening, Macready is 'by no means sanguine, I lament to say, on its success'. He discusses the play with the author again on 22 and, together with Forster, on 28. On 29 RB brings the newly revised text. To Macready he looks 'very unwell, jaded and thought-sick'. On 30 Mr Osbaldiston of Covent Garden agrees to produce the play without delay.

April
3 (Mon) – 4 Discussion of alterations to *Strafford* continues between Macready and RB, as between Macready and Forster on 5 and between all three on 7. On 8 the play is read, in RB's presence, to the actors. Further uncertainties, cuts, alterations and discussions follow over the next few days. On 12 Macready finds Forster 'very much out of humour with Browning'. On 14, after Forster has lost his temper with him (as he often does with other friends), RB says that he will withdraw the play; Forster then persuades him not to. Further revisions and delays are agreed. Macready continues

much concerned over 'this delicate affair of Browning'. He wishes, especially after RB comes to breakfast 'very pale' and over-excited on 22 that he could withdraw the piece, but feels he must go on out of loyalty. On 23 he still feels that it will fail utterly in the theatre, but is determined to do what he can in the last rehearsals.

29　EBB's 'Dear unknown friend! esteemed Canary!' is sent to ten-year-old Mary Hunter.

May

1　(Mon) RB's *Strafford; a Tragedy*, dedicated to Macready, is published by Longman at 4s. (at the publisher's expense) and given its first performance at Covent Garden. At the dress-rehearsal that afternoon RB expresses 'extreme delight' at Macready's portrayal of Strafford. But he regards the other actors, apart from John Vandenhoff as Charles I and Helena Faucit as Lady Carlisle, as incompetent and remains convinced that too little was done to ensure the success of the production. There are three more performances between now and 9. To Macready's surprise they are relatively well received.

June

2　(Fri) EBB agrees with MRM that *Pickwick Papers* is admirable. She is struck by Dickens' 'wonderful indi- viduality … No one could pass a character of his in the street without bowing'.

12　RB sees Macready as Hamlet at the Theatre Royal, Haymarket.

14　Monclar arrives in London and sees RB and his family a number of times between now and August.

20　William IV dies and is succeeded by Victoria.

26　Probable first meeting of RB and Charles Dickens in Macready's dressing-room after a performance of *The Bridal* (an adaptation by Macready and Sheridan Knowles of Beaumont and Fletcher's *The Maid's Tragedy*).

28   MRM, having become editor of *Findens' Tableaux*, asks
      EBB to write a poem ('A Romance of the Ganges') to
      illustrate the 'pretty superstition' shown in an engrav-
      ing of William Daniell's *Hindoo Maidens Floating
      Lamps*, which she has already seen at the Royal
      Academy.
Late in the month RB abandons his plan for a tragedy on
the death of Marlowe on hearing of R.H. Horne's *The Death
of Marlowe* (published in *The Monthly Repository* in August).

July
  1   (Sat) Writing to Euphrasia Fanny Haworth, RB says
       that he has 'many half-conceptions, floating fancies',
       on what will become the theme of *The Return of the
       Druses* (1843): some 'subject of the wild and most pas-
       sionate love. ... [G]ive me your notion of a thorough
       self-devotement, self-forgetting; should it be a woman
       who loves thus, or a man?' Alternatively he is looking
       for a subject for a historical tragedy – probably for
       the work which became *King Victor and King Charles*
       (1842).
  1   EBB's 'The Young Queen' (*Seraphim*) is published in
       The Athenaeum.
  8   Her 'Victoria's Tears' (*Seraphim*) is published in *The
       Athenaeum*.
  17   She sends 'A Romance of the Ganges' to MRM, refus-
       ing the offered £5 payment.

August
  9   (Wed) RB tells Monclar that *Sordello* is 'now under-
       going a final revision'.
  10   By about this date EBB has finished *The Seraphim*.
  19   In a letter to Lady Margaret Cocks she discusses works
       by Goethe and Schiller, of whom she likes especially
       the latter. (But on 12 March 1839 she tells MRM that
       'there is more essential genius in Goethe's mysterious
       Faustic growlings than in Schiller's most eloquent elo-
       quence'.) She began studying German last summer
       with her brothers Bro and Henry (1818–96).

September
29 (Fri) EBB is working on 'Isobel's Child' (*Seraphim*), 'a wild tale'.

October
Publication of *Findens' Tableaux: a Series of Picturesque Scenes of National Character, Beauty, and Costume* (dated 1838), including EBB's 'A Romance of the Ganges' (*Seraphim*).
21 (Sat) John Forster, reviewing *Findens' Tableaux* in *The Literary Gazette*, mentions favourably, and quotes the whole of, 'A Romance of the Ganges'.

November
4 (Sat) On the occasion of the christening of the son of William and Anne Dow RB writes (at least apparently impromptu) 'A Forest Thought'.

December
23 (Sat) He visits Harriet Martineau and tells her that *Sordello* 'will soon be done now'. She notes that he 'must choose between being historian or poet. Cannot split interest'.
23 Death in Jamaica of EBB's uncle Samuel Moulton-Barrett. He leaves her both money and shares in the ship 'David Lyon'.

1838

January
2 (Tues) Dickens and his friend the novelist Harrison Ainsworth meet RB at Covent Garden.
20 Forster and RB dine with Macready.

April
7 (Mon) RB sees Macready in Byron's *The Two Foscari* at Covent Garden.
13 He sails for Trieste on the brig 'Norham Castle', intending to finish *Sordello* 'among the scenes it describes'. His brief travel-diary (see *Correspondence* 4, xi–xiii) records landmarks passed en route including Cape

Finisterre (24), Cape St Vincent (27; see 'Home-Thoughts, from the Sea', line 1 – but the poem is more likely to date from during or after RB's voyage to Italy in 1844), and the Straits of Gibraltar (29).

At about mid-month the Barretts move to 129 Crawford Street and then to 50 Wimpole Street.

May

12 (Sat) RB's ship passes Pantelleria island and then Malta (13), Sicily (14–16), Otranto (20), and Brindisi (23), before anchoring at Trieste (31) whence he sets off for Venice by steam-boat.

Late in the month EBB tells HSB that she has 'just finished a very long barbarous ballad' – 'The Romaunt of the Page'. (The version she will send to MRM for *Findens' Tableaux* on 6 June contains revisions prompted partly by John Kenyon's charges of obscurity; it will be further revised for *1844*.)

June

1 (Fri) RB arrives in Venice and takes lodgings at Casa Stefani, Calle Giacomuzzi, San Moise 1139.

6 EBB's *The Seraphim, and Other Poems* is published at 7s. 6d. by Saunders and Otley, the first work to be published under the name Elizabeth B. Barrett. She and her father consider *The Seraphim* the best poem she has yet written. The form is, she told Kenyon this spring, 'rather a dramatic lyric, than a lyrical drama, and the subject, the supposed impression made upon angelic beings by the incarnation & crucifixion – a very daring subject, which suggested itself to me whilst I was *doing* that translation of Aeschylus'. Most reviewers find it over-ambitious, preferring the 'Other Poems', but their general conviction of her 'genius' and potential extends her reputation considerably.

17 RB goes on from Venice to Treviso (17), from which he walks to Bassano (18) and Asolo (19–23; on 20 he visits the Rocca, the 'Turret' of *Pippa* Part Three). He reaches Vicenza on 24 and Padua on 25 before returning to Venice on 26, at which point his diary ends.

July

15   (Sun) About now RB arrives back in London. He has travelled from Venice, he tells Haworth, via Verona, Trent, Innsbruck, Munich, Würzburg, Frankfurt, Mainz, Cologne, Aachen, Liège, and Antwerp (where the original inspiration for 'Master Hugues of Saxe-Gotha' (*MW*) possibly occurs to him in an organ-loft). He also tells Haworth that during his travels he composed only 'a scene in a play, jotted down as we sailed thro' the Straits of Gibraltar' – on 29 April – and four lines for Book Three of *Sordello*, addressed to Haworth as 'Eyebright'. (See *Sordello*, III. 967 ff.)

23   He sees Macready as Kitely in Ben Jonson's *Every Man in his Humour* at the Theatre Royal, Haymarket.

August

4   (Sat) He sees Macready as Thoas in Thomas Noon Talfourd's *The Athenian Captive* at the Haymarket.

EBB is told by Dr William Chambers that for the sake of her lungs she must go to a warmer place than London. She has been ill, in varying degrees, for much of the time since September 1837. On 25 she sets off by boat for Plymouth and arrives in Torquay on 27 with her brothers Bro and George, sister Henrietta, and new servant Elizabeth Crow. They stay at first with the family of EBB's aunt Jane Hedley. (EBB remains in Torquay until September 1841. In a letter to MRM of 12 November 1841 she remembers it as 'a dancing, fiddling cardplaying gossipping place, dissipated and full of ghastly merriment' and invalids. Her view is coloured, however, by her desperation to leave the town after Bro's death in July 1840.)

October

EBB's 'The Romaunt of the Page' (*1844*) is published in *Findens' Tableaux* for 1839.

1   (Tues) The Barrett group in Torquay (except George) moves to 3 Beacon Terrace.

12   EBB's 'A Sabbath on the Sea' (finished by late September; revised as 'A Sabbath Morning at Sea' in

1850) is published in *The Amaranth: a Miscellany of Original Prose and Verse*, edited by T.K. Hervey.

December

16   (Sun) He attends a private reading of Bulwer Lytton's play *Richelieu* at Macready's house.
24   Dickens, Forster and RB come to watch Macready rehearse the pantomime *Harlequin and Fair Rosamond*.

At the end of 1838 or the beginning of 1839 RB is probably aware of Fanny Kemble's play *An English Tragedy*, submitted to Macready on 19 December and based on the real story of Lord de Ros, which will also influence RB's *The Inn Album* (1875).

1839

January

About now RB is involved in some editorial capacity with the *Poetical Works of Shelley* published by Edward Moxon this spring.

26   (Sat) EBB's 'L.E.L.'s Last Question' (*1844*) is published in *The Athenaeum*.

February

1   (Fri) RB sees Bulwer-Lytton's play *The Lady of Lyons* (with Macready as Claude Melnotte), a possible source of Part Two of *Pippa*.

March

27   (Wed) RB, Harriet Martineau, and Thomas Carlyle dine with Macready.

April

10   (Wed) EBB tells MRM that she finds Harriet Martineau's novel *Deerbrook* 'all on a level ... I long for a flood to break it into pieces, because in that case beautiful and noble bits of landscape might be extracted for high admirations'.

June

24 (Mon) EBB tells HSB that she has begun a 'wild and wicked ballad' – 'The Legend of the Browne Rosarie'.

August

3 (Sat) In a letter to MRM, she discusses and defends what some feel to be her 'obstinate proclivity' towards bringing religion into her poems. 'The deepest mysteries … are, as approachable by lofty human thoughts & melted human affections, – poetical in their nature.' If the religion seems to intrude, this must be the result of her own lack of skill and not of any 'unfitness of the subject'.

Late this month EBB writes 'A Dream'.

This summer is the most likely date for RB's composition of *Pippa*. He will tell Alexandra Orr that he 'was walking alone, in a wood near Dulwich, when the image flashed upon him of some one walking thus alone through life; one apparently too obscure to leave a trace of his or her passage, yet exercising a lasting though unconscious influence at every step of it; and the image shaped itself into the little silk-winder of Asolo, Felippa or Pippa'.

September

5 (Thurs) Macready reads RB's *King Victor and King Charles* and tells him that it is 'a *great mistake*'.

At about mid-month EBB sends Richard Hengist Horne manuscripts of 'The Madrigal of Flowers' (in *1844* as 'A Flower in a Letter') and 'The Cry of the Human' (*The Boston Miscellany of Literature and Fashion*, November 1842).

October

1 (Tues) She moves to 1 Beacon Terrace, Torquay.

Her 'A Dream' and 'The Legend of the Browne Rosarie' (revised as 'A Child Asleep' and 'The Lay of the Brown Rosary' in *1844)* are published in *Findens' Tableaux* for 1840.

1840

January

EBB's father sends her Shelley's *Essays, Letters from Abroad, Translations and Fragments* (1840). By 6 February she has read it and and 'were it not for the here and there defilement of his atrocious opinions [it] would have very deeply delighted me'. On 14 June 1841 she tells MRM that Shelley 'froze in cold glory between Heaven and earth, neither dealing with man's heart, beneath, nor aspiring to communion with supernal Humanity, the heart of the God-Man'.

February

15 (Sat) EBB's 'The Crowned and Wedded Queen' ('Crowned and Wedded' in *1844*) is published in *The Athenaeum*. (Queen Victoria married Prince Albert on 10.)

March

 7 (Tues) RB's *Sordello* (6s. 6d.) is published by Edward Moxon at his father's expense. At the end three Dramas are announced as 'Nearly ready': these are *Pippa*, 'Mansoor the Hierophant' – the first version of *Druses* – and *King Victor*.

23 RB, responding to Alfred Domett's comments on *Sordello*, maintains that he is not '"Difficult on system" so much as guilty of forgetting that publication implies a general audience as well as the author's "lovers"'. Chris Dowson's kind words on the poem show that 'after all, writing unintelligible metaphysics, is not voted as bad as murder'.

24 Probable date of EBB's 'Lessons from the Gorse' (see 23 October 1841).

April

Her 'A Night-Watch by the Sea' appears in *The Monthly Chronicle*.

News arrives of the death in Jamaica on 17 February of her brother Samuel Moulton-Barrett.

In April or May RB sends 'Mansoor the Hierophant' to Macready.

May

5   (Fri), 8, 12, 15, 19 and 22 He attends Thomas Carlyle's lectures on *Heroes and Hero-Worship*.

In June–July, in response to Macready's criticisms, RB revises and expands *Druses* (formerly 'Mansoor the Hierophant').

July

EBB's 'The Lay of the Rose' ('A Lay of the Early Rose' in *1844*) is published in *The Monthly Chronicle*.

4   (Sat) Her 'Napoleon's Return' (on the decision to allow the emperor's reburial in France) appears in *The Athenaeum*. It will be revised for *1844* as 'Crowned and Buried'.

11   EBB's brother Bro is drowned while sailing in Tor Bay. His body is not recovered until 4 August. She is seriously ill for several months and for the rest of her life prefers to speak about her loss as little as possible, even to RB.

31   RB delivers to Macready his revised *Druses*.

August

3   (Sat) Macready reads *Druses*; 'with the deepest concern I yield to the belief that he will *never write again* – to any purpose. I fear his intellect is not quite clear'. On 9 RB partly accepts Macready's opinion of the likely failure of the play in the theatre but also defends it vigorously to him. They discuss the faults of the play and of *Sordello* on 12 and again on 27, when RB 'really *wearied* me with his obstinate faith ... of his eventual celebrity' and 'self-opinionated persuasions upon' *Druses*.

September

15   (Tues) Macready reads parts of the play again but remains unimpressed with this 'mystical, strange and heavy' piece.

December
RB's family moves to Hatcham, New Cross, to a larger, three-storey house (once a farmhouse) with a substantial garden, stable and coach-house. On the third floor are RB Senior's extensive library and RB's small study in what is believed once to have been a secret Roman Catholic chapel. Early this month *The Poems of Geoffrey Chaucer, Modernized*, edited by R.H. Horne and dated 1841, includes EBB's 'Queen Annelida and False Arcite' and 'The Complaint of Annelida to False Arcite'.

17   (Tues) EBB's first mention of her projected dramatic collaboration with Horne, later known as *Psyche Apocalypté*. (Horne first suggested this in the early part of 1840. EBB manages, with some difficulty, to avoid meeting him; liaison on *Psyche* is entirely by letter.) She is now clearly recovering from the physical collapse which followed Bro's death.

1841

January
7   (Thurs) Flush, son of MRM's spaniel of the same name, arrives in Torquay as her gift to EBB.

At about mid-month EBB writes to Horne on her ideas for *Psyche*: 'the terror attending spiritual consciousness ... seems to admit a certain grandeur & wildness in the execution'; 'There are moments when we are startled at the footsteps of our own Being, more than at the thunders of God.' Discussion of the project continues frequent in their correspondence over the next few months but it is effectively abandoned by the end of the year.

February
21   (Sun) RB completes a first draft of 'The Cardinal and the Dog' (eventually printed in *Asolando*).

March
He meets Alfred Tennyson for the first time at one of Richard Monckton Milnes' breakfasts.

April

c. 10 (Sat) – 15 RB, while in bed with a fever, composes a tragedy mainly inspired by Euripides' *Hippolytus* but on his recovery writes down only 'Artemis Prologuizes' (*DL*).

Towards the end of the month RB's *Pippa Passes* (price 6d.) is published by Edward Moxon at the expense of RB Senior. It is the first of the eight pamphlets of *Bells and Pomegranates*, the title of which is finally explained in a note to *A Soul's Tragedy*, in the eighth and final pamphlet, in 1846: 'I only meant ... to indicate an endeavour towards something like an alternation, or mixture, of music with discoursing, sound with sense, poetry with thought. ... [S]uch is actually one of the most familiar of the many Rabbinical (and Patristic) acceptations of the phrase'. *Pippa* is accompanied by an Advertisement explaining that it is meant 'for the first of a series of Dramatical Pieces ... and I amuse myself by fancying that the cheap mode in which they appear will for once help me to a sort of Pit-audience again' (the sort of audience which, he says, applauded *Strafford*). It is dedicated to Thomas Noon Talfourd.

June

21 (Mon) Thomas Carlyle writes to RB about his reactions to *Sordello* and *Pippa*: 'you seem to possess a rare spiritual gift ... to unfold which into articulate clearness is naturally the problem of all problems for you'. Probably his next work should be prose since 'One must make a *true* intellectual representation of a thing, before any poetic interest that is true will supervene'.

July

15 (Thurs) EBB writes to MRM about *Pippa*. It is hard to understand – '"Pippa passes" ... comprehension, I was going to say!' In her next letter to MRM, on 17, she is more approving. 'The conception of the whole is fine, very fine – & there are noble, beautiful things everywhere to be broken up & looked at'; RB asserts himself 'with a strong and deep individuality; and if he does it in Chaldee, why he makes it worth our while to get

out our dictionaries!' She also finds in his work, however, 'a want of harmony, particularly when he is lyrical'.

August

21   (Sat) EBB's 'The House of Clouds' (*1844*) is published in *The Athenaeum*.

September

Early this month RB leaves with Macready the manuscript of *A Blot in the 'Scutcheon*, written probably at some time during the preceding year.

1   (Wed) EBB, Arabel, and Elizabeth Crow set off from Torquay, travelling slowly by carriage to 50 Wimpole Street, where they arrive on 11.
26   Macready reads *A Blot* with John Forster. Some time between now and autumn 1842 Forster approaches Dickens for his opinion of the work. (See 25 November 1842.)

October

Early in the month MRM tells EBB that 'The Romaunt of the Page' is 'a tragedy of the very deepest and highest order' and 'by far the finest thing that you have ever written; and I do entreat and conjure you to write more ballads or tragedies ... like that; that is to say, poems of human feelings and human actions. They will be finer, because truer, than any "Psyche" can be'.

11   (Mon) RB and Macready call on Dickens, who is recovering from the removal of a fistula.
23   EBB's 'Lessons from the Gorse' (*1844*) is published in *The Athenaeum*.
28–30   MRM visits EBB in London.

November

18   (Thurs) She is considering writing an epic poem on either Napoleon (as MRM has suggested) or Joan of Arc, to whom she inclines; 'Perhaps my original sin of mysticism is struggling towards her visions'. She also tells MRM about her mainly enthusiastic reaction to

J.H. Jung-Stilling's *Theory of Pneumatology*, prompting discussion of spirits and related matters with MRM in their next few letters.

December

RB dines with Thomas and Jane Carlyle.

About now he writes the first version of 'In a Gondola' (*DL*), at John Forster's house in Lincoln's Inn Fields, to accompany Daniel Maclise's painting *The Serenade*. On actually seeing the painting, some time before 5 February 1842, he revises the poem to make it less 'jolly'.

5   (Sun) RB, Maclise, Macready, Ainsworth and others dine with Talfourd.

1842

January

8   (Sat) EBB's 'Three Hymns, Translated from the Greek of Gregory Nazianzen' are published in *The Athenaeum*.
12   Charles Wentworth Dilke, editor of *The Athenaeum*, suggests to EBB the account of 'poetical literature' since Chaucer which he will publish as *The Book of the Poets* in June and August.
20   She assures MRM that she couldn't give up poetry for prose if she tried; 'I cannot remember the time when I did not love it.' All her griefs cannot shake this love, and she is now more bent than ever on working 'into light … not into popularity but into expression … whatever faculty I have'. In the same letter she mentions RB and Horne as 'true poets' undervalued in *The Athenaeum*.

February

26   (Sat) The first part of EBB's *Some Account of the Greek Christian Poets* appears in *The Athenaeum*.
27   RB and Forster dine with Macready.

March

5   (Sat), 12, 19 The remaining parts of *Greek Christian Poets* appear in *The Athenaeum*.

5   An early review of *King Victor* appears in *The Spectator*, suggesting that some copies may be circulated before the official publication date.

12 RB's *King Victor and King Charles* – the second volume of *BP* – is published at 1s. by Edward Moxon. The cost to RB Senior is about £16.

26 RB and Macready dine with John Kenyon. Soon afterwards John Kenyon tells EBB that RB would like to meet her and suggests that he should bring him to Wimpole Street. She refuses.

April

26 (Tues) RB writes to Macready to know what his intentions are with regard to the intended presentation of *A Blot*, concluding with a suggestion that he should withdraw the work and print it at once. Macready delays his decision partly because he is waiting for Dickens' verdict on the play.

30 Alfred Domett leaves England for New Zealand. RB's 'Waring' (*DL*) is written soon afterwards.

In April or May he writes 'The Pied Piper of Hamelin; a Child's Story' for Macready's son Willie (1832–71), at home with a bad cough, to illustrate. Willie also does drawings for 'The Cardinal and the Dog'. 'The Pied Piper' is a late addition to *DL*, needed because without it there are too few poems to fill the sixteen-page pamphlet.

May

14 (Sat) Kenyon sends AT's *Poems* (1842) to EBB. She tells Kenyon on 15 that she feels none of the new poems equals 'Oenone'; she acknowledges the working of the intellect in the later poems, but misses 'something of the high ideality, and the music that goes with it' of the earlier. Later in the year she several times expresses her growing belief in AT as a 'true poet'. RB writes to Domett about the volume on 13 July; he dislikes the revision and omission of earlier poems but particularly admires 'Locksley Hall' and 'St Simeon Stylites'.

20 He goes to a party at Macready's with Forster, Carlyle, Kenyon and many others.

22 He tells Alfred Domett that he is bringing out 'a few songs and small poems' – *DL* – 'which Moxon advised me to do for popularity's sake!'

June

4   (Sat) The first part of EBB's *The Book of the Poets* is published in *The Athenaeum*.

July

RB's review of R.H. Wilde's *Conjectures and Researches Concerning ... Torquato Tasso* (1842) is published anonymously in *The Foreign Quarterly Review*. (Later it will be known as the *Essay on Chatterton*.)

August

6   (Sat) and 13 The fourth and fifth instalments of EBB's *The Book of the Poets* are published in *The Athenaeum*. She is paid £20 for the completed work and suggests, on 22, sending it to her harrassed and financially troubled friend MRM. The offer is politely declined.

27 EBB's review of Wordsworth's *Poems, Chiefly of Early and Late Years* appears in *The Athenaeum*.

September

17 (Sat) Her 'A Claim in an Allegory' (revised as 'The Claim' for *1844*) appears in *The Athenaeum*.

RB, on a visit to Sir John Hanmer at Bettisfield Park, Flintshire, probably completes Part the First (lines 1–215) of 'The Flight of the Duchess' (see April 1845) .

October

Early this month Benjamin Robert Haydon lends EBB his 'Wordsworth on Helvellyn'. On 17 (Fri) she sends him the poem published in *The Athenaeum* on 29 as 'Sonnet on Mr. Haydon's Portrait of Mr. Wordsworth' (reprinted in *The New York Daily Tribune* on 26 November and in *The New York Weekly Tribune* on 3 December; *1844*).

19 She defends RB's work to the dubious MRM, finding in *Pippa* a unity and nobleness of conception which outweighs 'all the riddles in riddledom'. On 7 December

she speaks of herself, too, as writing 'from riddledom' and on 5 November, defending herself and RB, tells MRM that great writers from Aeschylus and Pindar to Wordsworth and Coleridge have been 'obscure by the nature of the thought' where lesser writers have been 'obscure through imperfection of the expression'.

November
EBB's 'The Cry of the Human' (revised for *1844*) is published in *The Boston Miscellany of Literature and Fashion*.

25 (Fri) Dickens sends Forster his verdict on *A Blot*: 'It is full of genius, natural and great thoughts, profound, and yet simple and beautiful in its vigour ... And I swear that it is a tragedy that MUST be played ... And if you tell Browning that I have seen it, tell him that I believe ... that there is no man living (and not many dead) who could produce such a work'. Forster does not tell RB this, but Dickens' response probably persuades Macready that he should go ahead with the piece.

26 RB's *Dramatic Lyrics – BP* no. III – is published at 1s. by Edward Moxon. The Advertisement says that the poems 'come properly enough, I suppose, under the head of "Dramatic Pieces"; being, though for the most part Lyric in expression, always Dramatic in principle, and so many utterances of so many imaginary persons, not mine'.

During late autumn EBB discusses French novelists in several letters to MRM, expressing admiration for Balzac and Hugo mixed with moral scruples – partly for her correspondent's sake – particularly about Sand.

December
EBB's 'I tell you, hopeless grief is passionless', 'When some beloved voice', 'What are we set on earth for?' and 'The woman singeth at her spinning-wheel' are published in *Graham's Magazine* through her American correspondent Cornelius Mathews. (The poems appear in *1844*, revised, as 'Grief', 'Substitution', 'Work', and 'Work and Contemplation'.)

Schloss's Bijou Almanac for 1843 includes EBB's 'Introductory Stanzas' and 'The Duchess of Orleans'.

Late this month she first suggests to Edward Moxon the collection of her work which will become *1844*.

1843

January

RB's *The Return of the Druses. A Tragedy in Five Acts* – *BP* no. IV – is published by Edward Moxon at 1s.

In the first week of the month Haydon begins to send EBB his *Autobiography*. He often also sends her paintings and sketches to inspect.

  4 (Wed) EBB dates 'The Maiden's Death' (see March) and sends it to James Russell Lowell in response to a request for contributions to his short-lived periodical *The Pioneer*. She also sends two poems which he does not use, 'That Day' (*1844*) and 'Sonnet. Imperfect Manifestations' ('Insufficiency', *1844*).

25 Macready begins work on *A Blot*. On 28, he reports, the cast laugh at the play when the prompter reads it to them. Various discussions and disagreements between actor and playwright follow. By 1 February it has been decided that Samuel Phelps rather than Macready will play Lord Tresham, a fact later widely credited with the play's relative failure in production.

February

EBB writes 'The Lost Bower' (*1844*).

  6 (Mon) RB, frustrated with what he perceives as Macready's unsupportive approach to *A Blot*, sends the text to Moxon to print.

Phelps has fallen ill and it seems that Macready will after all play Tresham, but when he is in the midst of preparing it, on 10, Phelps announces that he must and will do it. RB, resisting further alterations proposed by Macready, declares himself perfectly satisfied with Phelps' portrayal.

The exasperated Macready can 'only think Mr. Browning a very disagreeable and offensive mannered person'.

11   RB's *A Blot in the 'Scutcheon. A Tragedy, in Three Acts –
      BP* no.V – is published by Edward Moxon at 1s. This
      evening and on 13 and 15 the play is performed at
      Drury Lane. (The production is well received but audi-
      ences dwindle rapidly; box-office receipts drop from
      £188 on the first night to £76 on the last.) RB remains
      convinced that Macready has been less than commit-
      ted to the play and the production, and cordial rela-
      tions come to an end until September 1852.

14   Having been given *A Blot* by John Kenyon, EBB writes
      to MRM of RB as 'a master in clenched passion … con-
      centrated passion … burning through the metallic
      fissures of language'.

Between about now and April RB writes *Colombe's Birthday*
with a view to having 'another actable play' put on by
Charles Kean.

March

In either February or March Moxon tells EBB, through
Kenyon, that he would like to publish her poems.
Her 'The Maiden's Death' is published in *The Pioneer.*
Haydon and EBB exchange a series of letters on the rela-
tive merits of Wellington and Napoleon. She champions the
latter.

 4   (Sat) RB writes 'There's a sisterhood in words' in the
      album of Helena Faucit, who played Lucy, Lady
      Carlisle in *Strafford* and Mildred in *A Blot.*

18   He snubs Macready in the street (according to
      Macready's diary).

25   Discussing 'The Dead Pan' (*1844*) with Kenyon, EBB
      mounts a vigorous defence of religion in poetry (cp. 3
      August 1839); the poem itself was conceived as an
      answer to Kenyon's paraphrase from Schiller 'The
      Gods of Greece' (in the Countess of Blessington's
      Keepsake for 1843).

April
4   (Tues) Wordsworth becomes Poet Laureate. RB's 'The Lost Leader' (*DRL*) may be inspired by this event or by Wordsworth's first official appearance at court on 25.

May
EBB expresses the belief, in a letter to Horne, that, for all his virtues, RB's worst fault is 'a want of *harmony* … spiritual & physical' (cp. 15 July 1841). Against her claim that he lacks music Horne writes '(Wonderfully wrong)'.
19   (Fri) RB has been shown the manuscript of EBB's 'The Dead Pan' by John Kenyon. He returns it with a note praising its 'famous versification', and Kenyon delights EBB by sending her the note.

June
24   (Sat) EBB's review of Horne's *Orion* is published in *The Athenaeum*.
29   RB is present at a dinner for the Devonshire House Sanatorium with Dickens (who is a member of the committee), Macready, Forster, Procter, Maclise and many others.

July
EBB's 'The Soul's Expression' (*1844*) appears in *Graham's Magazine*.
22   (Sat) Her 'To Flush, My Dog' (1844) – 'some very light cobwebby verses' – is published in *The Athenaeum*.

August
Her 'The Cry of the Children' (*1844*) is published in *Blackwood's Edinburgh Magazine*. It originated in her reading about the Commissions on children's employment in 1842–3, and especially the official report by her correspondent Horne.
EBB's 'Seraph and Poet' (*1844*) is published in *Graham's Magazine*.
She is angered by Dickens' treatment of America in *Martin Chuzzlewit* (1843–4).

September

Her 'The Child and the Watcher' (*1844*) is published in *Graham's Magazine*.

13 (Wed) Flush is stolen while walking with Elizabeth Crow. Negotiations between her brothers and 'the Fancy', a criminal organisation led by one Taylor, temporarily founder when Mr Barrett finds out about them, but the dog is eventually recovered on 15 following payment of £5.10s.6d.

October

EBB's 'Catarina to Camoens' (see 17 November 1831; revised for *1844*)) is published in *Graham's Magazine*.

 2 (Mon) She tells MRM that 'The Dead Pan' will be saved for publication in *1844* because Kenyon and 'perhaps I myself' think it 'superior to any preceding poem of mine'. She has also written over eight hundred lines of 'A Vision of Poets' (*1844*).

 4 Horne writes to ask EBB for a biographical sketch (provided) and a portrait (refused) for the volume he is to edit, *A New Spirit of the Age*. She insists that the death of Bro must not be alluded to in the work (cp. January 1852). On 17 Horne asks her also to contribute an account of Harriet Martineau and Anna Jameson, and on 20 of Wordsworth and Leigh Hunt. Between now and February 1844 she also works on accounts of Monckton Milnes and Carlyle and contributes to, or revises, parts of the essays on Landor, Tennyson, and others.

November

EBB begins work on 'A Drama of Exile', developed initially from an earlier fragment, 'The First Day's Exile from Eden'. The poem is finished in spring 1844.

December

27 (Wed) She has read Dickens' *A Christmas Carol* and tells MRM that she thanks the writer 'in my heart of hearts' for the scenes involving Bob Cratchit and Tiny Tim.

1844

January
EBB's 'The Lady's Yes. A Song' (*1844*) appears in *Graham's Magazine.*

February
8 (Thurs) She receives revises of *A New Spirit*, returning most of the sheets by 12. At mid-month she and RB both, unaware of each other's involvement, provide 'mottoes' for the chapters.

March
EBB's 'Loved Once' (revised for *1844*) appears in *Graham's Magazine.*
5 (Tues) *A New Spirit of the Age*, edited by Horne, is published by Smith, Elder. EBB is annoyed at Horne's treatment of her in the same essay as the poet Caroline Norton, and at many aspects of his version of her biography, which departs from the account she sent him to portray her as a reclusive, learned invalid.
She hangs in her room the engravings, given her by Horne, used for the *New Spirit* portraits of Harriet Martineau, RB (removed for his visits in 1845–6), Carlyle, Tennyson and Wordsworth.
9 Charles Kean hears *Colombe's Birthday* read and offers RB up to £500 on condition that the play is not produced for about a year and is not published in the meantime. RB, anxious not to lose his 'hold, such as it is' on his public – he has published nothing since February 1843 – refuses and sends the play immediately to press.
20 EBB begins sending material for *1844* to Moxon.

April
c. 20 (Sat) RB's *Colombe's Birthday. A Play, in Five Acts – BP* no. VI – is published by Edward Moxon at 1s.

May
Elizabeth Wilson (1817–1902) starts work as EBB's lady's maid in succession to Elizabeth Crow, who left in April

having become pregnant by, and married, the Barretts' butler William Treherne.

June

RB's 'The Laboratory (Ancien Regime)' and 'Claret and Tokay' (both in *DRL*) are published in *Hood's Magazine*.

10 (Mon) – 17 MRM stays in lodgings in Chapel Street, London, seeing EBB frequently.

18 EBB writes to thank HSB for a gift of Cyprus wine. At around the same time, presumably, she writes 'Wine of Cyprus' (*1844*), addressed to HSB (as she tells him in a letter of 31 July).

22 Forster's review of *Colombe's Birthday* in *The Examiner*, concluding that 'we abominate his tastes as much as we respect his genius', breaks his friendship with RB. They will be reconciled in the autumn of 1845.

July

RB's 'Garden Fancies' (revised for *DRL*) is published in *Hood's Magazine*.

22 (Mon) EBB writes 'The Romance of the Swan's Nest' and sends it to John Kenyon with 'A Rhapsody of Life's Progress' (both included in *1844*).

23 Execution, near Cosenza, of Attilio and Emilio Bandiera, who led an abortive rebellion against the King of Naples in June. Their high rank and defiant death makes Italian nationalism a much talked of topic just before RB's departure for Italy in August, the more so following Giuseppe Mazzini's proof that the British government opened his post, including sensitive communications from the Bandiera brothers. Mazzini, who will admire 'Italy in England' in *DRL*, is often credited with at least partly suggesting the speaker of this poem. (EBB refers to the death of the Bandiera brothers in *CGW* I.879–85.)

27 EBB writes 140 lines to 'finish a ballad-poem called "Lady Geraldine's Courtship" which was lying by me'. She does this because Moxon wants the first and second volume of *1844* to be of equal length; this poem

will end the first volume. It is a '"romance of the age"', she tells HSB, treating of railroads, routes, and all manner of "temporalities"' and radical enough to offend the conservative reviews.

August
RB's 'The Boy and the Angel' (*DRL*) is published in *Hood's Magazine*.
EBB's 'Pain in Pleasure' (*1844*) is published in *Graham's Magazine* and 'Insufficiency' (*1844*) in *The United States Magazine and Democratic Review*. Publication has been arranged by Cornelius Mathews.

12 (Mon) RB departs for Italy. During the voyage to Naples he may conceive or compose 'Home-Thoughts, from the Sea' (known by this title from 1849; in *DRL* it is the third section of 'Home Thoughts, from Abroad') and 'How They Brought the Good News from Ghent to Aix' (*DRL*). Later he will believe that the second of these poems was written at sea off Sicily in 1838, but it seems more likely to be a fruit of the 1844 journey.

13 EBB's *Poems* is published at 12s. in two volumes by Edward Moxon, dedicated to her father and with a preface which includes a declaration that 'Poetry has been to me as serious a thing to me as life itself; and life has been a very serious thing'. On 14 she sends a copy to Thomas Carlyle as one 'holding his genius and his teaching in high respect'. (In his letter of acknowledgement he suggests that one of her 'insight and veracity' should write prose in 'these days of crisis'.) Copies are also sent to Wordsworth, Landor, Martineau, and Leigh Hunt. *1844* is widely and on the whole approvingly reviewed, attracting much notice in America as well as Britain.

September
RB lands at Naples.

16 (Mon) Harriet Martineau writes to EBB about her cure by Mesmerism, her published accounts of which begin to appear in *The Athenaeum* from November. EBB

engages in frequent discussion of the topic with Martineau and other correspondents. With MRM she also enters on a fresh period of intensive discussion of French literature; her greatest enthusiasm is for Balzac, to read whom 'is a plunge into social life, *done in the imagination*' (9 October) and whose 'wonderful great-ness in making the ideality, real, – & the reality, ideal, I take to be unequalled among writers' (28 December). But French novels reflect the 'scepticism of opinion' and 'license of manners' of French society and are safe only for 'eclectic' readers.

17   By now she has 'half finished' the new version of Aeschylus' *Prometheus Bound* which will eventually be published in *1850*.

22   In a letter to Robert Shelton Mackenzie, who is seeking information for a proposed Dictionary of Living Authors, EBB says that she has lived in her Art since childhood and 'tasted in it her sweetest experiences', indeed almost 'her only very sweet experiences, ... of life under the earthly aspect'.

October

RB travels south from Naples at the end of September or beginning of October, crossing the Piano di Sorrento (setting of 'Italy in England') and visiting on 4 'Those isles of the syren, your Galli', Amalfi, and possibly Salerno.

1   (Tues) *A Drama of Exile, and Other Poems* – the American edition of EBB's *1844* – is published ($3) by Henry G. Langley, New York.

8   EBB tells Kenyon that she has 'a great fancy for writing one day a longer poem of a like class [to 'Lady Geraldine's Courtship'], ... a poem comprehending the aspect and manners of modern life, ... and flinching at nothing of the conventional'.

19   Flush is stolen again and recovered on 21 on payment of £7. Alfred Barrett negotiates with the dog-stealers on EBB's behalf; the whole affair is concealed from their father.

Probably in mid or late October RB goes to Rome, including the Protestant Cemetery to see the graves of Keats and Shelley, the Grotto of Egeria decribed by Byron in *Childe Harold* Canto Four, and the church of Santa Prassede (near Santa Maria Maggiore) – the 'St Praxed's' of 'The Tomb at St. Praxed's' (later 'The Bishop Orders his Tomb ...'). At the end of this month or the beginning of November he goes to Pisa, Livorno – where he meets Edward John Trelawny, friend of Shelley and Byron – and Florence, where he perhaps conceives 'Pictor Ignotus'. Many of the poems included in *DRL* in 1845, including those just mentioned, are written during or soon after this journey.

November
RB travels home probably through Germany and the Low Countries.
EBB writes 'To G.B.H.' – Rev. George Barrett Hunter, who is now a regular visitor at Wimpole Street (see 22 August 1845).
2   (Sat) MRM visits EBB.
23   The writer and art historian Anna Brownell Jameson (1794–1860) visits her for the first time.

December
30   EBB, thinking towards the long poem which will even-tually become *Aurora Leigh*, says to MRM that she wants to write 'a Don Juan, without the mockery & impurity', a poem which has unity but also allows 'philosophical dreaming & digression'.

1845

January
By the first few days of the month EBB has read *Vestiges of the Natural History of Creation* (1844), by Robert Chambers (published anonymously).
3   (Fri) In response to Henry Chorley's discussion of 'Poetesses' in *The New Quarterly Review* for January, she reflects on the lack of true 'poetesses' before Joanna

Baillie. The correspondence continues; on 7 she tells Chorley that 'I look everywhere for grandmothers and see none ...'

10   RB writes to EBB for the first time. While he was in Italy Kenyon gave a copy of *1844* to SB in which, some time ('last week') after his return, he came across the reference to the 'deep-veined humanity' of his work in 'Lady Geraldine's Courtship'. It is Kenyon who has persuaded him to write. While claiming that the poems have become so far part of him that he cannot, at the moment, give reasons for his admiration, RB celebrates their 'fresh strange music, the affluent language, the exquisite pathos and true new brave thought'; 'I do, as I say, love these Books with all my heart – and I love you too'.

13   In his second letter to EBB, RB contrasts their work: 'You speak out, *you*, – I only make men and women speak – give you truth broken into prismatic hues, and fear the pure white light, even if it is in me'. (Cp. the letter of 11 February: 'I never have begun ... "R.B. a poem"'.) In her reply, on 15, she praises his ability to deal both with abstract thought and human passion and his 'masculinity'.

18   EBB has recently read and enjoyed Paul de Kock's farcical *Mon Ami Piffard* (1845); by 20 she is reading Balzac's *Modeste Mignon*.

20   The Leeds Ladies Committee of the national Anti-Corn-Law League is considering asking her to write a poem for their Bazaar in May. The official request comes on 8 February. Although she has great sympathy for the cause, she writes to refuse on 10 February, deferring to the opinion of her father and Kenyon, who fear too close a political association.

28   Anna Jameson comes to see her. They talk about Jameson's friend Lady Byron; she tries to persuade EBB to keep an open mind about the wife against whom, with Napoleon's Marie-Louise, she has always had the strongest feelings. Another topic of conversa-

tion is *Vestiges of Creation*; EBB is not eager, she tells Kenyon on 29, to accept the notion of people as developed monkeys.

February

4   (Wed) Writing to MRM, she delights in *Modeste Mignon* and Balzac's use of language, like a poet, to coil up 'a thought into a word'. She objects, however, to his apparent scorn for poets and literary men as opposed to other artists and men of genius. She is now in the midst of the 'gorgeous extravagances' of Frédéric Soulié's *Les Mémoires du Diable* (1837–8).

11 RB's first mention of *Luria*, in a letter to EBB, as conceived but largely still to be written down. He works on it during the next few months and then again from late October, sending her each act as he completes it.

18 RB sends 'The Tomb at St Praxed's' to Frederick Ward, sub-editor of *Hood's Magazine*. The poem is 'a pet of mine, and just the thing for the time – what with the Oxford business' (i.e. the Oxford Movement).

27 EBB tells RB about her incipient idea for what will eventually become *AL*: 'a sort of novel-poem', completely modern and 'running into the midst of our conventions, and rushing into drawing-rooms and the like "where angels fear to tread"'. By this date EBB's revised translation of Aeschylus' *Prometheus Bound* is almost finished. (She also describes to RB the 'monodram' or monologue of Aeschylus which will later sometimes be published as his.) He discusses the play at some length in his letter of 11 March.

March

About now RB writes 'Home Thoughts, from Abroad' ('Oh, to be in England …'); the title is devised in response to EBB's suggestion of 4 October that the 'spring-song' needs one which will enable readers 'to catch your point of sight'. RB's 'The Tomb at St. Praxed's (Rome, 15–)' (*DRL*; 'The Bishop Orders his Tomb in St. Praxed's Church' in *1849*)

appears in *Hood's Magazine*, followed in April by Part the
First (lines 1–215) of 'The Flight of the Duchess'.

3   (Mon) MRM visits EBB.

5   EBB assures RB that she is *'essentially better'* and has
    been for several winters.

19 She has just finished Hans Christian Andersen's *The
    Improvisatore: or, Life in Italy* (translated by Mary
    Howitt, 1845). She likes its sense of 'inner life' and its
    descriptions of Italy.

20 EBB writes to RB about the disadvantages of her
    secluded life. When she seemed likely to die she
    thought with 'some bitterness' how she 'had stood
    blind in this temple I was about to leave', had seen no
    human nature and no great mountains or rivers; she
    was like 'a man dying who has not read Shakespeare ...
    and it was too late!' She would like to exchange her
    knowledge of books for 'some experience of life and
    man'. (But according to RB, on 15 April, 'all you gain by
    travel is the discovery that you have gained nothing,
    and have done rightly in trusting to your innate ideas'.)

31 RB mentions Anacreon in a letter to EBB. His
    'Transcriptions' from the *Anacreonta* are possibly com-
    posed about now.

April
(?) RB writes the first version of 'Saul' (*DRL*; completed in
MW, 1855).

During the first two weeks of the month EBB translates the
first canto of Dante's *Inferno* and begins work on translations from the Greek poets for inclusion in the proposed
'Classical Album' of Anne Thomson.

14 (Mon) Over the last few days she has been reading
    Stendhal's *Le Rouge et le noir* (1830); it is a work of dark
    and deep colouring which, she claims to MRM, she
    would mention only to her. It has 'ridden [her] like an
    incubus'.

At about the end of the month RB begins 'England in Italy'
(*DRL*; 'The Englishman in Italy' from *1849*).

16 EBB states and explores her belief in poetry as *'Truth in relation, perceived in emotion'* in a letter to Sara Coleridge.

26 EBB has completed most of the translations for the 'Classical Album' and sends them to Anne Thomson. (Some of the remaining work is done between now and 1 May.)

30 RB, responding to EBB's recommendation of Andersen's *The Improvisatore* and the extracts he has read in reviews, contends that 'Italy is stuff for the use of the North, and no more'; there is almost no poetry in Italian literature (cp. 19 May 1866), even Dante.

In late April and early May EBB, who supports the bill to endow Maynooth College, a Roman Catholic institution in Ireland, is angered by the intolerance of those, especially Dissenters, who oppose it.

May

2 (Fri) She has just begun reading Balzac's *Esther*, part of *Splendeurs et misères des courtisanes* (1838–47).

3 RB (to EBB) somewhat qualifies his remarks against Italian literature of 30 April, exempting Dante now, but still contrasting the vagueness of Italian poems – their generalised flowers and fruits, for instance – with what northern poets make of the same materials. (Several of the natural features he refers to figure in 'England in Italy' which he is still writing or has just completed.)

Early this month he suffers from bad headaches and is forced to cancel a number of social engagements.

14 EBB has read and corrected the proof of Horne's 'The Carnival at Cologne' for the June number of *The New Monthly Magazine*.

20 RB's first visit to EBB at 50 Wimpole Street, from 3.00 to 4.30. This is, initially, the usual length of visit. (EBB's brothers are absent until about 6.00 and her father until 7.00.) 'In February 1846 the visits began to creep over two hours; by March, two and a half or two and three-quarter hours is standard; the first three-hour

visit is no. 74 (Thursday, 24 June 1846)' (Karlin, pp. 76–7). There were to be ninety-one visits in all, the last on 11 September 1846.

22   RB writes a letter (subsequently destroyed) containing a declaration of love. EBB's reply (23) insists that she will refuse to see him again if the matter is mentioned further. ('The Lost Mistress' (*DRL*) is perhaps to be associated with this turn of events.) RB apologises (24) but argues skilfully that she has misunderstood his intentions; she accepts this and apologises (25), and the relationship is thus able to continue.

31   They meet for the second time.

June

EBB's review of Cornelius Mathews' *Poems on Man* appears in *Tait's Edinburgh Magazine*.

5   (Thurs) At their third meeting RB probably gives EBB his notes on her revised *Prometheus*.

9   She is carried downstairs with no ill effects. She is feeling gradually stronger.

11 and 18   RB visits EBB.

26   MRM visits EBB.

28   RB's sixth visit to Wimpole Street. Later he goes with an (unidentified) friend to see François Vidocq's museum of murder-weapons.

July

3   (Thurs) EBB confides in RB (admitting that she would not like Anna Jameson or Harriet Martineau to hear her say it) that she believes there to be 'a natural inferiority of mind in women – of the intellect ... not by any means, of the moral nature – and that the history of Art and of genius testifies to this fact openly'. Women's minds are quicker in movement but less deep and powerful. The only woman who seems to justify any other conclusion is 'that wonderful woman George Sand' with her breadth and scope, her magnanimity, her instinct towards an ideal purity. (EBB's two sonnets to Sand appeared in *1844*.)

5 RB shows her 'The Flight of the Duchess', lines 216–95.
7 EBB leaves Wimpole Street for a brief carriage-ride to Regent's Park. During the winter of 1845–6 she will become much more active and by the late spring of 1846 will go out regularly.
10 and 16 They meet for the eighth and ninth times.
11 RB is reading, or has recently been reading, Disraeli's *Sybil* (1845).
*c.*16 EBB's father and aunt Jane Hedley are discussing the idea of sending her to Alexandria or Malta for the winter.
c. 18 RB sends her the manuscripts of the poems published in *Hood's*. She admires 'The Tomb at St Praxed's' most and 'Claret and Tokay' least. Her comments (in letters and in more detailed notes) contribute extensively to the poems as revised for *DRL*.
24 and 30 RB visits EBB.

August
EBB's *Sonnets from the Portuguese* is written between now and early 1846. (All except the last two sonnets are probably finished by December.)
6 (Wed) RB visits EBB. He gives her a first version of 'England in Italy'. Between receiving her favourable comments (in letters of 7–13 August) and completion by 13 October, he introduces revisions and adds the conclusion in which 'Men meet gravely to-day/ And debate, if abolishing Corn-Laws/ Be righteous and wise'.
11–16 They discuss Sand's *Consuelo* (1842), which EBB already knows and RB finishes on 14 or 15. He is wearied by the novelist's statement of characters' qualities where a dramatist must '*make* you love or admire his men or women' on the grounds only of what the audience sees and hears. Aspects including a lack of logic make *Consuelo* like 'what in conventional language with the customary silliness is styled a *woman's-book*'. EBB agrees with some of what he says but argues that the novel is unrepresentative of the author

and that the 'want of practical logic' is 'a human fault rather than a womanly one'.

12   RB visits EBB.

22   Rev. George Barrett Hunter, a disappointed suitor of EBB who has known her since her time in Sidmouth in the early 1830s and now irritates her with his apparently contemptuous attitude to women, follows RB upstairs in Wimpole Street 'in rather an ill temper'.

26   RB visits EBB. On 27 he sends her the manuscript of the first version of 'Saul' (*DRL*).

30   He sends her his second, allowed declaration of love.

30   Dr Chambers, consulted by EBB, encourages her in her scheme of wintering abroad for her health, perhaps in Pisa.

September

1   (Mon) RB visits EBB. She sends him Mary Shelley's *Rambles in Germany and Italy* (1844), which he finds commonplace and lacking in interesting detail.

8 and 12   RB visits EBB.

16   She explains to him that her father will not 'tolerate in his family (sons or daughters) the development of one class of feelings'.

20   RB goes (having been sent a ticket by Forster – an opening for their reconciliation next month) to Dickens' production of *Every Man In His Humour* at the Royalty Theatre, Dean Street; he thinks highly of the performances (including Forster's Kitely and Dickens' Bobadil) and costumes.

22   RB visits EBB.

She attempts to persuade her father that she should go abroad for the winter. He tells her, in 'a hard cold letter', that she has permission to do so. On 24 she tells him (according to her letter of this date to RB) that 'my prospects of health seemed to me to depend on taking this step, but that through my affection for him, I was ready to sacrifice those to his pleasure if he exacted it – only it was necessary ... to understand definitely that the sacrifice *was* exacted by him and *was* made to him. ... And he would not answer *that*. ... For his part, he washed his hands of me altogether'. At about the same time he ends his nightly visits to pray with her.

25   RB's letter to EBB mentions the idea of marriage; in her reply of 26 she acknowledges that she returns his love.

26   His twentieth visit. He comes again on 30.

October

EBB's 'Sonnet: a Sketch' (see June 1847; *1850*) and 'Wisdom Unapplied' (*1850*) appear in *The Christian Mother's Magazine*.

3   (Fri) and 9 RB visits.

12   George Barrett tackles the patriarch on the subject of EBB's going abroad and is told that she may go if she pleases, but it will be 'under his heaviest displeasure'. As a result 'I *do not go to Italy*' (partly to avoid exposing George and Arabel, involved in her Italian plans, to the same displeasure). She realises now that 'I had believed Papa to have loved me more than he obviously does'. This increasing alienation from her father has a 'catalytic effect ... on the block which she had established between herself and Browning' (Karlin, p. 107).

13   *DRL* is sent to press.

16   RB visits.

18   He receives proofs of the first half of *DRL* and on 20 sends them on, with corrections, to EBB (whose suggested emendations they incorporate). Among other poems she singles out for praise 'The Lost Leader' ('worth all the journalizing and pamphleteering in the world!') and 'The Flight of the Duchess', which 'appears to me more than ever a new-minted golden coin'. The remaining proofs reach RB on 27 and EBB on 28; she has most to say about 'The Glove', for which 'all women should be grateful, – and Ronsard, honoured, in this fresh shower of music on his old grave', 'though the chivalry of the interpretation, as well as much beside, is so plainly yours'.

21 and 28　　RB visits EBB.
31　　MRM pays her a rather garrulous five-hour visit. EBB successfully directs conversation away from the subject of RB.

EBB's recent reading has included Balzac's *Les Paysans* (1844), Sand's *Le Meunier d'Angibault* (1845), and the last volume of Eugène Sue's *Le Juif errant*.

November

3　　(Mon) RB visits EBB.
6　　RB's *Dramatic Romances and Lyrics – BP* no. VII – is published by Edward Moxon at 2s. (As for nos I–VI, the expense to RB's father is about £16.)
8 and 13　He visits EBB.
13　　Giuseppe Mazzini writes to RB. He has 'read, re-read and made his friends read' 'Italy in England' in *DRL*; men like RB can do much to excite sympathy in England for 'our condition and our cause'. Mazzini encloses his *Ricordi dei fratelli Bandiera* (1844; see 23 July 1844), which RB passes on to EBB on 20.
13　　She reads the first act of *Luria* twice before she sleeps. It is 'all life', she tells RB on 14. Such 'living poetry', she says on 8 December, is to be contrasted with the 'polished rhetoric' of Talfourd's *Ion*. She also begins to write the more detailed notes on *Luria* which she will give RB on 19 March 1846.
15　　RB is at the second (command) performance of the Dickens *Every Man In his Humour* in the presence of Prince Albert.
19　　RB's fortieth visit.
22　　W.S. Landor, to whom he has sent a copy of *DRL*, publishes 'To Robert Browning' in *The Morning Chronicle*, declaring that

> Since Chaucer was alive and hale,
> No man hath walkt along our roads with step
> So active, so inquiring eye, or tongue
> So varied in discourse.

25 RB visits EBB.

December

She starts work on 'The Runaway Slave at Pilgrim's Point', partly inspired by 'a subject for a poem about a run away negro' (with a contrastingly anti-slave emphasis) given her many years earlier by her cousin Richard Barrett (d. 1839).

1 (Mon) RB delivers the second act of *Luria* to EBB. He comes again on 6.

10 He attends a concert of sacred music by Eliza Flower; he is probably also present at its earlier performance on 22 November.

11 and 17 He visits EBB.

20 She has read Dickens' *The Cricket on the Hearth* and tells RB that it is 'with considerable beauty ... extravagant' and not one of his more successful pieces.

22–24 Writing to RB about the 'system' of conventional love-relationships, she attacks male vanity and hypocrisy; women 'act as if they had to do with swindlers' because of the system by which men try 'to force a woman to stand committed in her affections ... before *they* risk the pin-prick to their own personal pitiful vanities'. 'Men make women what they are'.

23 RB gives EBB the third act of *Luria*. She continues to write notes on it. They next meet on 29.

1846

January

3 (Sat) RB visits EBB.

5 She is sent a copy of the American writer Margaret Fuller's *Woman in the Nineteenth Century* (1845) and presumably reads it soon afterwards, although she tells RB that she hates 'those "Women of England" "Women and their mission" and the rest – As if any possible good were to be done by such exposition of rights and wrongs'.

8 RB visits.

8 or 9   EBB receives a copy of Edgar Allan Poe's *The Raven and Other Poems* (1845) which, as she has known for some time, is dedicated to her – rather mystifyingly as far as she is concerned. (Poe will send her a presentation copy, bound with his *Tales*, in mid-March.)

10   RB goes (as again on 16 April) to a private performance of 'theatricals' by Talfourd's son Frank (Francis, 1828–62). Also there are 'Dickens and his set'.

10   EBB, writing on the anniversary of RB's first letter, compares herself to 'one taken suddenly from a lampless dungeon and placed upon the pinnacle of a mountain'.

13   John Kenyon, who calls frequently on EBB, arrives, frustratingly, in the middle of RB's (fortieth) visit and they leave together. RB, as often during the courtship period, is suffering from headaches.

20   He delivers to EBB the fourth act of *Luria*. They next meet on 24.

28   He claims the fulfilment of her promise to marry him, 'say, at the summer's end'. She replies on 30 that 'if, in the time of fine weather, I am not ill' he will decide and she will make no difficulties.

29   RB visits EBB.

30   RB watches Charlotte and Susan Cushman as Romeo and Juliet at the Haymarket. He finds the playing – Romeo whining about Verona in broad daylight – exaggerated.

At the end of the month EBB is reading Carlyle's introduction to *Oliver Cromwell's Letters and Speeches* (1845). RB is reading the book in late March and is sent the second edition by Carlyle on 1 July.

February
Early in the month EBB experiments successfully with reducing her opium intake.

3   (Tues) RB visits her.

5   MRM visits her. EBB finds her once dear correspondent increasingly exhausting and limited, manages again to steer the conversation away from RB, and

doubts at least some of the scandals she reports of Horne. Although MRM is affectionate towards her she feels that 'if I were to vex her ... she would advertise me directly for a wretch proper'.

9   RB gives EBB the fifth act of *Luria*. She writes on 10, admiring the 'calm attitude of moral grandeur' of the work as a whole. But she feels that tightening is possible especially towards the end, and admits to some disappointment in Domizia, who might profitably be made a little 'more a woman'. RB agrees that Domizia is 'all wrong' in his reply of 11.

13   Having reread *Soul*, he tells EBB that its subject-matter and style are too 'unpopular' to form a worthy conclusion to *BP*; lately he has, besides, lost interest in dramatic writing.

14 and 18   RB visits EBB.

18   The philanthropist Sir Moses Montefiore (1784–1885) invites RB to join his mission to St Petersburg to help Russian Jews. He does not, to EBB's relief, seriously consider going.

20   Kenyon entertains RB, Procter, Henry Crabb Robinson and EBB's brother George. (RB and Crabb Robinson are among those at another Kenyon gathering on 9 March.)

22   W.J. Fox, at the National Hall of the Working Men's Association, Holborn, delivers his 'On Living Poets; and their Services to the Cause of Political Freedom and Human Progress – No. 10. Miss Barrett and Mrs [Sarah Flower] Adams'. Fox sees EBB as a poet of solitude and 'strong sense of invisible reality' and reads from 'Crowned and Buried', 'The Cry of the Human', and 'The Cry of the Children'. RB, reading the published version of the lecture (*The People's Journal*, 7 March) finds it 'inconceivably inadequate'.

23   He visits EBB. Later he goes (as again on 4 April) to a *soirée* given by the Marquess of Northampton as President of the Royal Society.

26   EBB tells RB that she feels 'an indisposition to setting about the romance' (the future *AL*) but has 'all in blots

and fragments ... verses enough to fill a volume done in the last year'.

26 Anna Jameson calls on her and offers to take her to Italy. Another visitor, Sarah Bayley, several times makes the same suggestion later in the spring.

28 RB visits EBB.

March

c.1 (Sun) She is reading the first volume of Sand's *Le Péché de M. Antoine* (1846). She tells MRM that she likes its sympathy for the masses but feels that human beings are too imperfect to realise Sand's egalitarian ideals.

3 Hearing from EBB that her father appeared displeased at his visit on 28 February, RB allows himself, unusually, to write about Edward Barrett's shocking unreasonableness. In her reply of the same day she attempts to explain his 'miserable misconception of the limits and character of parental rights'.

5 RB's fiftieth visit.

9 He brings EBB the first act of *A Soul's Tragedy*. She finds it 'vital' and a good balance for *Luria* (to RB, 10 March). He comes again on 14, 19, when she gives him her notes on *Luria*, and 23.

23 EBB sends Anne Thomson translations from Hesiod and the *Anacreonta* for her projected 'Classical Album'. She is working on Homer's parting of Hector and Andromache for the same compilation.

25 (and briefly on 26) Anna Jameson calls on EBB. She is still keen that they should go to Italy together, and expresses enthusiasm for RB's work. She now becomes a fairly regular visitor.

28 RB gives EBB the second act of *Soul* (having cut out 'a huge kind of sermon from the middle') together with proofs of *Luria* Acts I–II. The remaining *Luria* proofs reach her on 29. All this material, with notes on the first act of *Soul* and a few last suggested corrections for *Luria*, is returned to RB on 30.

April
1 (Wed) Following the conclusion, after much bloodshed, of the First Sikh War, EBB questions, in a letter to her brother George, Britain's right to an Indian empire.
2 RB visits her.
4 Final proofs of *Luria* and *Soul* reach RB.
4–10 EBB and RB disagree, in a series of letters, on the practice of duelling. At about this time RB probably writes 'Before' and 'After' (*MW*).
6 and 11 He visits her.
11 By now EBB has completed her two alternative translations of 'The Daughters of Pandarus' (*LP*) from *The Odyssey* to be used by Anna Jameson in *Memoirs and Essays Illustrative of Art, Literature, and Social Morals* (1846). Jameson reads them admiringly to RB when they breakfast together on 8 May.
13 RB's *Luria; and A Soul's Tragedy – BP* no. VIII – is published by Edward Moxon at 2s. 6d. and dedicated to W.S. Landor, 'a great dramatic poet'.
15 and 20 RB visits EBB.
20 RB visits Carlyle, who speaks unusually favourably of RB's recent work.
25 RB visits EBB.
26 She tells him about her enthusiasm for stories like those of Alexandre Dumas; listening to stories 'is a taste quite apart from a taste for literature'. On 28, agreeing with RB's enthusiasm for Balzac's use of recurring characters in *La Comédie humaine*, she praises his 'most wonderful faculty'; 'His French is a new language – he throws new metals into it'.
29 RB dines with Forster and Leigh Hunt.
30 RB visits EBB.

May
Probably this month she helps to edit 'Johnny Cheerful', an unpublished novel by Henrietta Barrett's suitor Surtees Cook.

4 (Mon) RB visits EBB.

5 She meets her correspondent Ellen Heaton (1816–94) for the first time.

5 RB and Anna Jameson are among the guests at a party with music given by Henry Chorley.

6 RB, Chorley, Alexander Kinglake, Richard Monckton Milnes and the poet Coventry Patmore are entertained by the Procters.

9 RB visits EBB.

11 He and Jameson go to an exhibition of prints by Marcantonio Raimondi, a pupil of Raphael. She has recently completed *Memoirs and Essays, Illustrative of Art, Literature, and Social Morals* (1846), and delivers a proof of its first essay ('The House of Titian') to EBB on 12. Partly because of Jameson's ideas and personality and partly because she speaks so well of each to the other, RB and EBB feel increasing affection for her.

11 EBB, Arabel, and Flush drive to Regent's Park where EBB surprises herself by walking a little. They go again on 21; by June she is going out quite frequently.

12 At a dinner given by his publisher Edward Moxon RB makes closer acquaintance with AT. Joseph Severn, Keats' friend, is also present and Shelley is one of the topics of conversation.

13 RB 'returns thanks' for the dramatists at the Royal Literary Fund Dinner.

14 and 18 He visits EBB.

14 In a letter to Anna Jameson (as in their conversations before and after this) EBB, while praising the eloquence and 'sympathy' of her *Memoirs*, disagrees with her view that art is not generally 'the medium of expression for the present Age'. She could believe this only if she could 'believe in an age without souls, … of a lopped, straightened humanity'. EBB expatiates on the point to RB on 16: art expresses the age only accidentally – 'essentially it is the expression of Humanity in the individual being'.

20   Anniversary of the first meeting of EBB and RB. About now, probably, she writes *Sonnets* xx ('Beloved, my beloved, when I think/That thou wast in the world a year ago …').

20   RB is presented by Dickens with a copy of his *Pictures From Italy* (1846). RB feels that it concentrates too much on the least interesting places before going on hurriedly, but remains 'readable and clever'. At the same time EBB is about to begin Dickens' book and is already reading *Notes on Naples and its Environs* ('by a Traveller', 1838), lent by RB. (At this time they sometimes imagine themselves living in or visiting Amalfi, mainly because of its mention in RB's 'England in Italy' and Landor's 'To Robert Browning'. Florence is felt to be too full of English, some of them objectionable parvenus. Ravenna, Pisa, Sorrento, and Salerno are among the other possible destinations mentioned.)

23 and 27   RB visits EBB.

26   Carlyle visits RB.

29   RB is at the Royal Academy Exhibition. He finds William Etty's picture of Circe and the sirens 'abominable'.

29   EBB goes with Arabel to Kew Gardens where, against regulations, she picks a pansy to send to RB.

June

Early this month RB is reading Machiavelli.

1   (Mon) RB visits EBB.

2   EBB, with Arabel, calls on their old family friend Mary Trepsack. The visit is another sign of renewed strength. In a letter written to RB later in the day she wonders whether perhaps she should precede him to Italy with a friend or they should leave marriage until next summer or autumn. He makes clear in his reply of 3 that yet more waiting would be intolerable.

2   RB dines with Kenyon and Landor and on 3 with Kenyon, Jameson and others. On 4, with W.M. Thackeray, Jameson, and Milnes, he is among guests at

the Procters' ball. (Macready is also present; RB ignores him.)

6   Seventieth meeting of RB and EBB.

7   EBB is reading Dumas' *Le Comte de Monte-Cristo* (1844–5).

11   RB visits EBB.

12   EBB visits Kenyon.

12   RB feels it unjust not to tell his parents about his intention of marrying. He also suggests that he should somehow obtain employment or a literary pension and that EBB should make over her money to her siblings. She continues, in her reply of the same day, to maintain the need for complete secrecy; as for the money, she will not 'put away God's gifts' intended perhaps for just this exigency.

13   Kenyon takes EBB to see the new Great Western locomotive in action.

14   Landor sends EBB his *Works* (1846). RB also receives a copy about now.

17   EBB, driving with Jameson in Regent's Park, tells her that she and RB know each other – a fact carefully concealed from her until now.

20   RB visits EBB.

22   EBB and Anna Jameson visit Samuel Rogers' art collection.

22   Haydon commits suicide.

24   RB breakfasts at Carlyle's with Countess Ida Hahn-Hahn. He has recently read the English translation (1844) of her novel *Gräfin Faustine* and found it 'a horrible book' for whose heroine with her 'irresistible longings' he feels only contempt.

25 and 29   RB visits EBB.

30   EBB is studying more books about Italy – John Forsyth's *Remarks on Antiquities, Arts and Letters* (1813) and Mariana Starke's *Travels on the Continent* (1820) – in search of an ideal home.

30   EBB and Arabel visit HSB at St John's Wood. They have not met for seven years. Seemingly unchanged,

he lectures her as in the past about the authenticity of Ossian.

July

2   (Thurs) MRM visits EBB. She is not very glad to see her and also dreads the imminent arrival of her aunt 'Bummy' and other relations in preparation for the wedding of EBB's cousin Arabella Hedley; she hates being with people who don't know and value RB, she tells him on 1. (She admits to pleasure at seeing her aunt, Jane Hedley, on 13 – RB would like her – and her uncle Robert Hedley, with whom on 17 she has an ostensibly jocular exchange about whether he will cast her off if she appears at his Paris home as a runaway en route for Italy.)

5   EBB learns that Haydon has left instructions that she should edit or arrange publication of the memoirs he has entrusted to her. On 7 RB ascertains for her from Talfourd, who is Haydon's executor, that the papers are legally the property of Haydon's creditors. She writes to Talfourd herself on 8 and eventually, on his advice, sends the memoirs to Haydon's family.

8, 11, 14   RB visits EBB.

15   She meets Arabella Hedley's bridegroom-to-be, James Bevan, and on this and subsequent occasions is bored or annoyed by his uncritical Puseyism and obsession with church architecture. She has begun to investigate the cost of different sea- and land-routes to Italy.

15   RB sees and is enthusiastic about the French actress Rachel as Racine's Phèdre at St James' Theatre.

18 and 21   He visits EBB.

22   She writes to him that 'you shall see some day at Pisa what I will not show you now', her first clear reference to *Sonnets from the Portuguese*. In her second letter of 22 she suggests to him that they should take her maid Elizabeth Wilson with them to Italy; at £16 per annum EBB judges her 'expensive' but very capable. He at once agrees.

25　RB visits EBB.

26　At his insistence she writes a statement that at his death she wishes her estate to be divided, in the first instance, between her sisters. (Originally he wanted this to take place on *her* death if she predeceases him.)

27　Forster and Moxon visit RB.

28　RB visits EBB.

28　Kenyon has told Anna Jameson that Mr Barrett will undoubtedly prevent EBB from going to Italy with her. Kenyon and the Hedleys are angry at Barrett's unreasonableness but at a loss how to alter the situation. Henrietta tells Kenyon – somewhat to EBB's dismay – that she must get to Italy without help from her friends and may 'surprise everybody some day'. Over the next few weeks RB often, and EBB quite often, have the impression that Kenyon has divined the real nature of their relationship.

29　EBB tells Fanny Dowglass that she is inscribing a book with two as yet unprinted sonnets (probably among those published in June and July 1847).

30　She goes with Arabel to see Westminster Abbey for the first time.

Probably in late July or August RB reads in a newspaper (incorrectly remembered as *The Times*) an account of constancy in misfortune which will provide the basis of his 'The Melon-Seller' in *Ferishtah* (1884).

August

Early in the month, in a letter to MRM, EBB writes against conventional marriages, where the glories of the wedding arrangements (her cousin Arabella's wedding is on 4) soon give way to misery. In love and marriage women are degraded, she tells RB on 12, by their exclusion from men's serious concerns.

1　(Sat) Mr Barrett returns home early during a heavy storm, concerned for EBB who has since her days at Hope End had a terrible fear of storms, and finds that RB has been in the house for some time. (He already knows that he calls, but not how often or for how long.) Highly displeased, Barrett later says to his daughter 'it appears, Ba, that *that man* has spent the whole day with you'. For her that day, 'the lightning … made the least terror'.

4　RB visits EBB.

5　She states her financial position to him: she has £8000 in government stocks, yielding around £40–45 quarterly income, and £200 annually (reinvested) from her share in the merchant ship *David Lyon*. Her greatest expense at present is morphine.

5　Anna Jameson calls on EBB and asks her if she has completely given up the idea of going to Italy. She says that she has not and hints at secrets to be revealed later.

6　Henrietta cries out in astonishment at how much better EBB looks than a few weeks ago. She herself says (to RB, 6 August) that, although she does not always feel strong, she has had no symptoms of illness all summer.

6　She visits HSB. Either now or soon afterwards he guesses and coaxes from her her secret and is highly approving.

6　RB is at the Procters' with Kenyon, Thackeray, Milnes, and Anna Maria Goldsmid (1805–89), 'a pleasant chatting Jewess'.

8　He visits EBB.

10　RB and SB go to St James' Theatre to see Rachel as Hermione in Racine's *Andromaque*.

11　RB visits EBB.

12　Mary Trepsack has guessed that EBB intends to marry and go to Italy, but cannot be told explicitly.

12　RB, Procter, and Thackeray are at Kenyon's; Thackeray invites the others to dine at the Garrick Club on 19.

14　RB visits EBB.

18　He tells her that 'Wine of Cyprus' is the poem by her which has affected him perhaps more profoundly than any other. 'There is so much of you in it' he adds on 19.

18   EBB speaks at least half-seriously of their going to
     Greece and Egypt at some later date.
20   RB visits her.
22   He has been rereading Thomas Moore's *Letters and
     Journals of Lord Byron* (1830). His old affection for Byron
     has revived. Places and things connected with him
     have always meant more to RB than Wordsworth,
     Coleridge and Southey combined.
22   EBB is visited by Jameson and visits HSB. (She sees
     Jameson again on 24 and HSB on 25.)
26   RB is to borrow £100 from his father to help with the
     cost of going to Italy. (He will not accept it as a gift.) 'If
     we are poor, it is to my father's infinite glory,' he tells
     EBB after his mother has given him an account of his
     father's principled conduct on St Kitts and afterwards
     (see 1812). He has never known much about this
     because RB Senior has 'an invincible repugnance' to
     talking about the matter.
29   RB visits EBB.

Discussion of routes, connections, and prices for Italy continues. Pisa is now more or less definitely settled on as the
final destination. After some hesitation EBB agrees, on 31,
that they should leave in September.

September

1   (Tues) Flush is stolen for the third time. He is eventu-
     ally ransomed on 5 after EBB, with a daring at one
     time unthinkable for her, has gone to Shoreditch with
     Wilson to arrange to see the kidnappers' leader, Taylor.
     Her brother Alfred (sometimes called 'Daisy', 1820–
     1904) having insulted Taylor, her brother Sette
     (Septimus, 1822–70) goes to Shoreditch and finally
     obtains Flush on payment of a ransom of 6 guineas. In
     his letters of 3–5 RB protests on principle against
     the paying of such ransoms. He is troubled with
     headaches and dizziness, for which on 6 his doctor
     prescribes a few days in bed, a little medicine, no food
     and much milk. He is well enough to go out by 8.

9   RB visits EBB, as again on 11 when, precipitated into action by Mr Barrett's announcement that the family will move during redecoration of 50 Wimpole Street, they meet to finalise their plans.

12 RB and EBB are married at 11.00 a.m. at St Marylebone Church. The witnesses are Elizabeth Wilson and RB's cousin James Silverthorne. The couple leave separately, RB going home while EBB calls on HSB and then goes with her sisters to Hampstead Heath before returning to Wimpole Street.

15 Mr Barrett announces that the family will move to Little Bookham in Surrey on 21.

19 Having met between 3.30 and 4.00 p.m.at Hodgson's bookshop, Great Marylebone Street, RB, EBB, Wilson (who has organised many of the practical details of EBB's departure), and Flush, take the 5.00 train to Southampton from Vauxhall and sail at 8.15 for Le Havre.

20 The Brownings arrive in Le Havre and take coach at 9.00 p.m. for Rouen.

21 They arrive at Rouen (1.00 a.m.) and Paris (10.00 a.m.), where RB leaves a note for Anna Jameson at the Hôtel aux Armes de la Ville de Paris. (With her niece Gerardine Bate she has set off on the European travels on which she suggested EBB should accompany her.) In the evening Jameson, quite astonished, comes to see them at the Hôtel Messageries and on 22, at her persuasion, they take a suite of rooms at her hotel. She tells Lady Byron that EBB is 'nervous, frightened, ashamed, agitated, happy, miserable'.

During their week in Paris the Brownings stay mostly in the hotel to help EBB recuperate from the journey, but also visit the Louvre and dine at restaurants.

21 A wedding announcement, giving no date, is printed in *The Times* (and other newspapers, some of which give 19 as the date).

28–29 The Brownings move on from Paris to Orléans with Anna Jameson and Gerardine Bate; on 29 EBB receives letters of severe condemnation from her father (who henceforth will consider her as dead) and her brother George and of encouragement and sympathy from her two sisters. John Kenyon's letter is also supportive; 'if the thing had been asked of me, I should have advised it'. From Orléans the group visits Bourges Cathedral.

October

2   (Sat) – 3 The journey continues to Lyon via Roanne.
6   EBB, RB, and companions, travel by Rhône steamer from Lyon to Avignon. On 7 RB, Jameson and Gerardine visit the Palais des Papes. On 8, with EBB, they go to the Fontaine-de-Vaucluse, associated with Petrarch and his devotion to Laura; EBB and RB sit on the rocks amid the spray. On 9 or 10 they leave Avignon for Marseille via Aix-en-Provence. By now Jameson, charmed by RB and impressed by EBB's selflessness and powers of endurance, is convinced that the marriage 'has been well done'.
11 Departure from Marseille on the steamer *L'Océan*, arriving at Genoa on 12 and at Livorno on the morning of 14, whence they travel by train to Pisa. Here, after a few days at Hotel Peverada, they take, on 18, 'three excellent bedrooms and a sitting room, matted and carpeted' in the Collegio di Ferdinando (near the cathedral and Leaning Tower) for a rent (later discovered to be expensive) equivalent to £1. 6s. 9d. a week. Jameson and Gerardine remain in Pisa until 4 November.

This month seven poems by EBB are published in *Blackwood's Edinburgh Magazine*: 'A Woman's Shortcomings', 'A Man's Requirements', 'Maud's Spinning' (subsequently 'A Year's Spinning'), 'A Dead Rose', 'Change on Change', 'A Reed', and 'Hector in the Garden'. This 'heap of verses' was 'swept from my desk' and belonged 'to old feelings and impressions'; their unexpectedly rapid publication is unfortunate, since her father and others may find some lines 'impudent' at this time. Her father no doubt refuses, however, even to look at the work of his 'dead' daughter. All the poems are included in *1850*.

November

5 (Thurs) EBB, writing to MRM, stresses RB's excellence as a husband and the way her own health is improving rather than declining as a result of marriage and travel: 'Mrs Jameson says, "she wont call me *improved*, but *transformed* rather.' Similar reassurances often figure in EBB's letters at this time.

EBB and RB find contemporary Italian literature, for example Massimo d'Azeglio's novel *Niccolò di Lapi* (1841), disappointingly dull and conventional. Most of the books obtainable in Pisa are translated from French or, occasionally, English.

They drive to the pine-forest where Byron and Shelley used to shoot. Pisan landscape, like Pisan society, however, soon comes to seem very limited.

December

23 (Wed) EBB sends 'The Runaway Slave at Pilgrim's Point', completed this autumn, to James Russell Lowell. It will be published in *The Liberty Bell*, a Boston anti-slavery compilation, in 1848 and, with revisions, in *1850*.

24 They go to midnight mass in Pisa Cathedral. EBB is shocked at the apparent irreverence of the congregation and the lack of religious instruction or conviction in the service.

1847

February

At the beginning of the month they are reading Stendhal's *Le Rouge et le noir* (1830). EBB first read it in spring 1845.

March

21 (Sun) EBB's first miscarriage, after five months of pregnancy (unperceived until near the end).

This spring RB begins work on corrections to *Paracelsus* for inclusion in *1849*.

April

20 (Tues) The Brownings move to Florence. They stay at the Hôtel du Nord before taking a lease for two months (later three) on rooms at 4222 Via delle Belle Donne for £4 a month. Among early visitors are Anna Jameson and Gerardine Bate, who arrive to celebrate Shakespeare's birthday with the couple on 23 and set off for England a week later.

EBB reads more works by Dumas *père*.

May

EBB's poems 'Life', 'Love', 'Heaven and Earth. 1845', and 'The Prospect. 1845' (all in *1850*) are published in *Blackwood's Edinburgh Magazine*.

June

Her sonnets on her sisters, 'Two Sketches', are published in *Blackwood's Edinburgh Magazine*, followed by 'Mountaineer and Poet' and 'The Poet'. The second 'sketch' – of Arabel – had already appeared in *The Christian Mother's Magazine* in October 1845. All three poems reappear in *1850*.

The Brownings have recently met the American sculptor Hiram Powers (1805–73), whose 1843 'Greek Slave' is the subject of a sonnet by EBB in *1850*. They have also met Isabella and Richard Belgrave Hoppner, who knew Byron and the Shelleys in Venice, and visited the Uffizi, the Pitti, Santa Croce, and other popular Florentine places.

July

14 (Wed) They travel to Pelago and the monastery of Vallombrosa, whose abbot, in spite of a letter of dispensation from the Archbishop of Florence, refuses to allow entry to a woman. Before returning to Florence on 17 EBB stamps her foot just inside the monastery door, 'profaning it for ever' perhaps.

20 A three-month lease is taken out on seven furnished rooms on the *piano nobile* of Casa (or Palazzo) Guidi,

including free entry to the Boboli Gardens, for £1. 1s. a week plus 9s. a month for the concierge.

September

12   (Sun) From the front windows of Casa Guidi (not the windows of their own apartment), the Brownings watch the procession of Florentines to the Pitti Palace to salute Grand Duke Leopoldo II's granting them the right to form a civic guard. The celebrations will inspire EBB to write Part One of *Casa Guidi Windows*.

October

17   (Sun) Having read *Pauline* in the British Museum and noticed the 'analogy of style and feeling' with *Paracelsus*, Dante Gabriel Rossetti writes to RB to ask whether he wrote it. RB is happy to admit this in his reply of 10 November and a foundation is laid for the friendship of 1851–72.

20   Unable to renew the Casa Guidi lease except by paying much more, RB and EBB move to 1881 Via Maggio at a rent of £5. 7s. a month. Dissatisfied – mainly because the rooms are too cold – they expensively break the lease and move (*c*.30) to rooms (with a rent of 'heaps of guineas') in Piazza Pitti, opposite the palace. Here EBB writes 'A Meditation in Tuscany' (subsequently *CGW*, Part One), starting probably in **November** or early **December**.

1848

This year 'The Runaway Slave at Pilgrim's Point' (revised for *1850*) is published in *The Liberty Bell*, a Boston anti-slavery compilation.

February

17   (Thurs) Grand Duke Leopoldo grants a constitution to the people of Tuscany . RB and EBB watch his arrival at the Pitti Palace from the opera 'in the midst of a "milky way" of [the celebrators'] waxen torchlights'.

24   Republic declared in France. Initially both EBB and RB
      are well disposed to it, but their enthusiasm is some-
      what dampened by suspicion of the communistic ideas
      expressed by Louis Blanc, Charles Fourier, and Pierre-
      Joseph Proudhon; the basis of the Brownings' political
      faith at this time is 'a strong trust in individual liberty
      and an equally strong distrust of attempts to legislate
      abstract, impractical programmes' (Gridley, p. 81).

March
In the first week of the month EBB, two months pregnant,
miscarries again.
Some time this spring she sends 'A Meditation in Tuscany'
to William Blackwood, intending it to be published in
Blackwood's Edinburgh Magazine. (See October.)

May
 9   (Tues) EBB and RB move from Piazza Pitti to their old
      suite in Casa Guidi, this time taking it – much more
      cheaply – unfurnished, at 25 guineas a year.
10   HSB dies. Probably late in the month EBB writes her
      three sonnets (*1850*) in memory of 'this excellent and
      learned man, enthusiastic for the good and the beauti-
      ful, and one of the most simple and upright of human
      beings'.

June
The killing of five thousand rebel workers in Paris increases
EBB's disillusion with the new Republic. RB remains some-
what more hopeful.

July
17   (Mon) The Brownings travel to Arezzo in the evening
      and on to Fano on 18 or 19. On each of their three days
      in Fano they go to see, at the church of Sant' Agostino,
      Guercino's 'The Guardian-Angel'. During the week
      they then spend in Ancona, RB writes 'The Guardian-
      Angel: a Picture at Fano' (*MW*). They go to Loreto for a
      day, then (*c.* 29) back north up the Adriatic coast to
      Senigallia, Fano, Pesaro, Rimini, and Ravenna (where

they spend an hour outside Dante's tomb), and to
Florence via Forlì on about **7 August** (Mon).

October

Early this month EBB hears from William Blackwood, to
whom she sent 'A Meditation in Tuscany' in the spring. He
thinks it 'grand' but beyond human comprehension and
wishes her to provide explanatory notes. The poem will
eventually be published, as *CGW* Part One, by Chapman &
Hall in May 1851.

November

RB, unwell for months with an ulcerated sore throat and
now feverish, is cured with the aid of the mixed eggs and
wine of 'Father Prout' (Rev. F.S. Mahony), the cynical journalist, talker, and drinker whom he has known since the
1830s and who persistently visits Casa Guidi in the
evenings of the following six weeks.

27   (Mon) – 29 RB's *A Blot* is performed at Sadler's Wells
     Theatre by Samuel Phelps, as again on 7–9 December
     and twice more in February 1849.

December

10   (Sun) Louis Napoleon Bonaparte is elected President
     of the French Republic. RB is, and will remain, suspi-
     cious of his motives. EBB has been hoping for a new
     strong French leader but is as yet unconvinced that
     Louis Napoleon – whom she will later vigorously
     support – is the man.

1849

January

In early or mid-month RB's *Poems*, comprising *Paracelsus*
and *Bells and Pomegranates*, is published by Chapman &
Hall. (RB has found Moxon too slow; Chapman will also
publish EBB, a much more attractive financial proposition.)
Alterations include extensive revision of the Introduction to
Pippa Passes, the change of the title of 'Italy' to 'My Last

Duchess. Ferrara', and detailed revisions in *Colombe's Birthday*.

RB and EBB read Charlotte Brontë's *Jane Eyre* (1847). EBB finds it interesting but overrated.

February

7 (Wed) Grand Duke Leopoldo, having withdrawn from Florence to Siena on 30 January, sails for Gaeta where he joins the decreasingly liberal Pope Pius IX. On 14 Mazzini arrives to lend support to Florentine republicans.

March

9 (Fri) Birth of Robert Wiedemann Barrett Browning (baptised on 26 June at the French Evangelical Protestant church; Wiedemann was the name of RB's mother). He will be known at first as Wiedeman (written thus); according to RB infant attempts to pronounce this name result in the Pennini or Penini (later Pen) adopted by his family and close friends. But Pen himself will later believe that 'in trying to pronounce "Nini" – the name Italians give their children' he stuttered 'P-n-n-n-nini'. Elizabeth Wilson becomes his nurse.

During the pregnancy EBB attempts, with RB's encouragement, to stop taking morphine.

18 Death of Sarah Anna Browning, RB's mother, after a heart-attack. The announcement of Pen's birth arrives when she is already unconscious. SB breaks the news gradually to her brother in a sequence of three letters, the first two pretending that their mother is only gravely ill.

23 Piedmontese troops are defeated by the Austrians at Novara. King Carlo Alberto abdicates and in other parts of Italy conservative regimes begin to be restored or to regain confidence after the liberal triumphs of 1847–8.

April

12 (Thurs) Francesco Guerrazzi, briefly dictator of the Tuscan republic, is overthrown.

The Brownings read Thackeray's *Vanity Fair* (1847–8). EBB finds it 'very clever, very effective, but cruel to human nature'.

May

5   (Sat) EBB watches from her windows in Casa Guidi as Austrian troops occupy Florence in support of the restoration of Leopoldo. (The troops will remain until the spring of 1855.) Around this time, possibly, she starts work on Part Two of *Casa Guidi Windows*. The bulk of the work is probably undertaken, however, in the autumn of 1850.

June

EBB and RB, looking for a cooler place in which to summer, spend five days visiting Carrara, La Spezia, Lerici (where they see Shelley's last home), Seravezza, and Bagni di Lucca. Here they meet their friends Eliza and David Ogilvy, fellow-tenants at Casa Guidi. Before returning to Florence the Brownings arrange to rent a house (Casa Valeri, Bagni Caldi) from 30 at £12 for four months.

30   (Sat) The family sets off for Bagni di Lucca. Here RB gradually recovers from his intense grief at the death of his mother.

In spite of the French suppression of the Roman Republic and restoration of Pius IX EBB is by now fundamentally convinced of Louis-Napoleon's integrity.

July

2   (Mon) RB writes to SB that for 'these last three months' he has been thinking of nothing but Mama and 'catching at any little fancy of finding something which it would have pleased her I should do'. One such thing, probably, would be *Christmas-Eve and Easter-Day* (see November).

This summer EBB shows RB the poems which will become *Sonnets from the Portuguese*. Moved and impressed, he persuades her to include them (with some revision) in *1850*. ('Future and Past', which appears separately there, becomes sonnet xlii in the 1856 *Poems*). The title alludes originally to Catarina, the 'Portuguese' of 'Catarina to Camoens', although EBB and RB are aware that readers are more likely – helping the fiction of the poems' anonymity – to take 'Portuguese' as referring to the language.

August
RB reads and EBB rereads Dumas' *Le Comte de Monte-Cristo* (1844–5). At about the same time they read the first volume of Chateaubriand's *Mémoires d'outre-tombe* (1849–50), which she finds 'curiously uninteresting'.

September
17   (Mon) Excursion, by donkey and pony, to Prato Fiorito. (See also 20 or 21 August 1853).

October
17   (Thurs) The Brownings return to Florence.
Probably in late October or November they meet the American writer Margaret Fuller, recently married to the Marchese d'Ossoli.

November
RB begins *Christmas-Eve and Easter-Day*. He intends to write 'a Christmas Story in verse' but finds it impossible to finish for Christmas. The thought of writing on Easter 'as *next* season' then comes to him and he writes the 'supplement or complement'.

December
22   (Sat) EBB's 'A Child's Grave at Florence' is published in *The Athenaeum*, following the death of fifteen-month old Alice Cottrell, daughter of the Brownings' friends (Count) Henry and Sophia Cottrell. RB organised the funeral.

1850

February
18   (Mon) By now EBB has sent the manuscript of *1850* to Chapman.

March

1 (Fri) RB sends 'Christmas-Eve' to Forster to pass on to Chapman. 'Easter-Day' follows on 9.

April

1 (Mon) RB's *Christmas-Eve and Easter-Day. A Poem* is published by Chapman and Hall (price 6s.) at the publisher's expense (for the first time in RB's career since *Strafford*). There are a number of favourable reviews but the work sells badly after the first few weeks; Chapman & Hall still have copies in January 1864.

6 Henrietta Moulton-Barrett marries Captain William Surtees Cook and is disowned by her father.

23 William Wordsworth dies.

June

1 (Sat) Henry Chorley is the probable author of a piece in *The Athenaeum* suggesting that to appoint a female Poet Laureate 'would be at once an honourable testimony to the individual, a fitting recognition of the remarkable place which the women of England have taken in the literature of the day, and a graceful compliment to the Sovereign herself' and that EBB is the most suitable candidate of either sex. (AT is appointed to the post on 19 November.) *The Athenaeum* is, however, generally hostile to the very existence of the Laureateship.

July

2 (Tues) RB visits Siena.

28 EBB suffers her most serious miscarriage, after three months of pregnancy. She is badly ill for ten days.

August

13 (Tues) News arrives of the drowning (19 July) of Margaret Fuller d'Ossoli and her husband and son, near the end of their journey to America.

31 With EBB still recovering from her miscarriage and Pen from sunstroke, the family travels to Siena by train. After a night in the city they move to the nearby Villa Poggio al Vento ('windy hill'), Marciano, where the invalids soon recover.

September

27 (Fri) RB translates Giambattista Zappi's sonnet on 'The "Moses" of Michelangelo' (in San Pietro in Vincoli, Rome) for 'Ba "for love's sake"'.

October

1 (Tues) The family move into Siena to see sights including the cathedral, Sodoma's *Crucifixion*, and the house of St Catherine, before returning to Florence on about 7. Probably soon afterwards, EBB begins her main period of work on Part Two of *CGW*.

26 EBB's 'Hiram Powers' "Greek Slave"' (*1850*) is published (anonymously) in *Household Words*.

November

1 (Fri) EBB's *Poems* is published by Chapman & Hall at 16s. It includes the bulk of *Seraphim* (much revised) and *1844*, recent periodical contributions, *Sonnets from the Portuguese* (with the related 'Insufficiency', 'Life and Love', and 'Inclusions'), and the revised *Prometheus Bound*.

15 She is reading *David Copperfield* (1849–50), which RB has already finished.

December

13 (Fri) By this date she has read Elizabeth Gaskell's *Mary Barton* (1848). It is powerful but sometimes tedious ('these class-books must always be defective as works of art'). She has also read AT's *In Memoriam* (*1850*), which is 'full of deep pathos and beauty'; here Tennyson 'appeals heart to heart, directly as from his own to the universal heart, and we all feel him nearer to us'. RB also approves.

1851

May

3 (Sat) EBB, RB, Pen and Wilson leave Florence (until November 1852). With David and Eliza Ogilvy they

travel to Venice (arriving probably on 7) by way of Bologna, Modena, Parma, and Mantua. In Venice EBB and RB go to San Marco, to a melodrama, and to performances of Verdi's *Attila* and *Ernani*. They talk to the superior of the monastery of San Lazzaro degli Armeni, who taught Byron Armenian. They go to a festa at Chioggia. EBB is enraptured with the city but RB is uncomfortable and sleepless and Wilson unwell. The Brownings disagree, as often later, on how Pen should be dressed: RB – with male pride, EBB tells Arabel – objects to the lace caps and ribbons which make people take his son for a girl.

31 *Casa Guidi Windows* is published at 6s. by Chapman & Hall. A number of reviewers regard it mostly as commonplace, diffuse, some equivalent of MRM's verdict: 'a dull tirade on Italian politics'. *The Literary Gazette*, on the other hand, admires her 'fine and original perceptions and ardent style'.

June
13 (Fri) The Brownings leave Venice and proceed to Padua (whence they go to Petrarch's house at Arquà), Milan (visiting the cathedral and Leonardo da Vinci's 'Last Supper'), Lakes Como, Lugano, and Maggiore, the St Gotthard Pass, and (on 24) Lucerne. Here they learn that, the ship *David Lyon* having yielded EBB less income (£50) than usual, they cannot afford to travel slowly to Paris via Cologne; they go on more directly via Basle and Strasbourg, arriving in Paris on 30, where they stay at the Hôtel aux Armes de la Ville de Paris. The seven rooms cost the equivalent of 5s. a day.

July
15 (Tues) – 20 At some time between these dates EBB and RB meet the Tennysons at the Hôtel de Douvres in Paris. (EBB meets AT, and both Brownings Emily Tennyson, for the first time.) The couples get on well. AT offers them the use of his house in Twickenham during their forthcoming visit to England.

22–23　The Brownings travel from Paris to London. They rent three small rooms at 26 Devonshire Street, near Wimpole Street, at £2 a week. Soon after their arrival RB goes to New Cross alone to see his father and sister for the first time since the death of his mother. Soon afterwards EBB comes to meet them; she and RB spend two days at the house. They both write to Mr Barrett seeking reconciliation but receive from him a 'violent and unsparing' reply accompanied by the letters, unopened, which EBB sent him from Italy. Reconciliation with her brothers in London, particularly George, is, however, achieved. (Stormie is in Jamaica.) During their stay the Brownings also make or renew personal contact with friends including John Kenyon, MRM, Anna Jameson (with whom they go to the Great Exhibition), John Forster, R.H. Horne, Fanny Kemble, and Thomas Carlyle. (EBB first meets the latter two in late July at Kenyon's house.) Probably at the end of July, perhaps later in the summer, Dante Gabriel Rossetti is introduced to the Brownings by the American poet and painter Thomas Buchanan Read, who has met them in Florence.

August

c. 2　(Sat) Henrietta, Surtees and their son Altham come to see the Brownings in London, staying until *c.* 18.

15　Joseph Milsand's authoritatively favourable review of RB's work, 'La Poésie anglaise depuis Byron, II – Robert Browning', is printed in *La Revue des deux mondes*. On 15 January 1852 it will be followed by Milsand's companion piece on John Reade, Henry Taylor and EBB, generally favourable to her but out of sympathy with writing on contemporary politics as manifested in *CGW*. The Brownings first meet Milsand (1817–86) in Paris at the end of 1851 or the beginning of 1852.

September

24　(Wed) They visit Samuel Rogers.

25   With Thomas Carlyle, they travel by train and ship to Dieppe and (26) Paris. They stay at the Hôtel aux Armes de la Ville de Paris.

October
Early this month RB begins work on what will later be known as his *Essay on Shelley* (see February 1852). About now the Brownings again see the Tennysons, who are on their way back from Italy.

10   (Fri) The Brownings move to a seven-room apartment at 138 Avenue des Champs-Elysées where the rent is 200 francs or £8 a month.

28   EBB's aunt and uncle the Hedleys, and their daughter 'Ibbet', who have just moved from Tours to Paris, visit them.

29   EBB and RB attend one of the receptions held by Lady Elgin, who shares EBB's interest in spiritualism. They go to her usually on Mondays; on Fridays they are often at Mme Mary Mohl's similar gatherings. RB, unlike EBB, is able to continue these visits after the onset of cold weather in November.

November
2   (Sun) Publication of Talfourd's 'Sonnet to Robert Browning; Suggested by a Sunset of Unusual Beauty' in *Household Words*.

RB's father and sister come to Paris (until about the end of the month). RB Senior reveals at least some of the details of his now cooled passion for a widow, Mrs Minny von Müller. He gives the impression (on the basis of which RB writes to her) that she is bothering him.

December
2   (Tues) – 4 Louis Napoleon Bonaparte leads a *coup d'état*. Some fighting continues until 10. EBB supports him fervently, while RB is much more suspicious. (See e.g. RB to George Barrett, 4 February 1852.) Bonaparte's action is supported by a large majority in the plebiscite held on 20.

4–5   RB finishes the *Essay on Shelley*.

The cold winter of 1851–2 causes or coincides with a sharp decline in EBB's health. Her persistent cough, breathlessness, congestion, chest pains, and fever may suggest 'acute bronchitis verging on bronchopneumonia' (Forster, p. 268).

1852

January

In old age RB will believe that, as a result of a New Year resolution to produce a poem a day, he wrote the *MW* poems 'Love Among the Ruins', 'Women and Roses', and 'Childe Roland to the Dark Tower Came', on 1 (Thurs), 2 and 3. But although ideas for these and other poems may originate in Paris, they are almost certainly written in Florence in 1853 onwards.

This month MRM offends EBB, temporarily but deeply, by raising the subject of Bro's death in her *Recollections of a Literary Life*: this was 'the shadow that had passed over that young heart', prostrating her with horror, grief, and 'by a natural but a most unjust feeling, that she had been in some sort the cause of this great misery'. On this subject, she explains to MRM in a letter probably of 21–22, she has never been able to bring herself to tell even RB how she feels.

February

   5   (Thurs) RB attends the official reception of the Comte de Montalembert into the Académie Française at the Institut de France and hears complimentary speeches between him and his political opponent François Guizot; in 'Respectability' (*MW*) 'Guizot receives Montalembert'.

  15   and   22 RB and EBB are received by George Sand. EBB discerns 'an intense burning soul' under her quiet manner; RB, who meets Sand again several times including once in the Tuileries gardens, is much less taken and EBB feels that it was good of him 'to let me

go at all after he found the sort of society rampant around her' – the sycophantic 'ill-bred' males.

Letters of Percy Bysshe Shelley. With an Introductory Essay, by Robert Browning is published by Edward Moxon. On 23 Moxon learns that the letters are forgeries and withdraws the book.

March

Philarète Chasles gives two lectures on EBB (RB is present at one) which include material elaborated from MRM's indiscreet revelations about the death of Bro.

Early this month George Sand sends tickets for her play *Les Vacances de Pandolphe*. RB goes but the weather is too cold for EBB to venture out.

14 (Sun) RB is introduced to Alphonse de Lamartine by Lady Elgin.

April

By now Joseph Milsand is spending every Tuesday evening with the Brownings.

c. 5 (Mon) RB and EBB see Dumas *fils' La Dame aux camélias* at the Vaudeville. They both cry and EBB has a headache for twenty-four hours afterwards. Writing to George on 13–14 May she defends the play against charges of immorality.

May

10 (Mon) EBB and Anna Jameson, after a three-and-a half-hour drive through the congested streets, watch the ceremonial restoration of eagles to regimental standards in the Champs-de-Mars.

19 Death of RB's cousin James Silverthorne. SB twice urges him to come to England for the funeral, but he fails to do so because of EBB's health (a cold has stirred up her 'old symptoms'). EBB claims to Arabel on 25 that SB has no real understanding of her brother. His 'May and Death' (*DP*) is probably written soon afterwards.

In the last week of the month EBB, in a group including Anna Jameson and Mary Mohl, attends the reception of the poet and playwright Alfred de Musset into the Académie Française at the Institut de France.

July

1 (Thurs) £800 damages are awarded against RB's father for breach of promise to, and defamation of, Milly von Müller. The scandal causes RB considerable pain and embarrassment.

5–6 The Brownings travel from Paris to London, where they rent an apartment at 58 Welbeck Street.

Henrietta and Surtees Cook come to visit them, leaving for home probably on 16 or 17.

17 RB and EBB dine at the Procters' with guests including Richard Monckton Milnes and Anna Jameson.

c. 20 RB escorts his father and sister to Paris where they are to live in order to avoid paying the £800 damages.

27 Jane Carlyle introduces RB and EBB to Giuseppe Mazzini.

August

Wilson has asked for a pay-rise from £16 to £20 a year. The Brownings refuse and she says that she must leave them. EBB is 'in tribulation about my child's nurse, and in bondage to the child consequently'. By 3 September, however, before going to her family in Yorkshire for three weeks, Wilson agrees to stay on.

21–23 RB and EBB meet Charles Kingsley at the house of John and Caroline Paine in Farnham. EBB is 'much struck by his originality and intenseness'. Together they visit the ruins of Waverley Abbey.

28 and 30 RB and EBB breakfast with Samuel Rogers.

September

1 (Wed) RB is introduced to John Ruskin by the poet Coventry Patmore. John and Effie Ruskin call soon afterwards and, probably on 13, RB and EBB go to 51 Denmark Hill to have lunch and see Ruskin's collection of works by J.M.W. Turner.

23 RB, writing a letter of condolence to Macready on the death of his first wife, effects a reconciliation with him.
25 Wilson returns from Yorkshire.

October
5 (Tues) RB attends the christening of Hallam Tennyson, delaying leaving London for a week, during which the family live at 15 Bentinck Street. At the christening he meets F.T. Palgrave (later known for his *Anthology*), with whom he will become more closely acquainted from the 1860s.
11 RB writes 'A Face' (*DP*) in the album of Emily Patmore, Coventry Patmore's first wife.
12 The family leaves for Paris, where they stay in the Hôtel de la Ville l'Évêque.
16 They watch Louis Napoleon's triumphal entry into Paris.
23 They leave for Florence. The return south has been necessitated by the recurrence of EBB's coughing from the last few weeks in London onwards, and made possible by financial aid from Kenyon. They travel by rail to Châlons, by river to Lyon (25), and by coach to Chambéry before crossing Mont Cenis.

November
c. 1 (Mon) They arrive in Genoa where, with EBB exhausted and ill, they spend ten days. After another night of travelling and a night in Pisa, they arrive in Florence by train on about 12.
Her health improves once she is re-established at Casa Guidi. RB finds Florence dull after Paris.

December
2 (Thurs) Louis-Napoleon becomes Emperor Napoleon III.

1853

January
1 (Sat) An anonymous bouquet of roses is delivered to EBB. RB's 'Women and Roses' (*MW*) is written now or

soon afterwards. Probably on the following day he writes at least some version or some part of 'Childe Roland to the Dark Tower Came'. (He will later believe that he wrote the entire poem in one day.) It comes upon him 'as a kind of dream' which has to be written 'then and there'.

29   Napoleon III marries Eugénie de Montijo in a civil ceremony, followed on 30 by a church wedding at Notre Dame. The reference to this in RB's 'A Lovers' Quarrel' (*MW*) gives an approximate date for at least some stage of its composition.

February

24   (Thurs) He tells Milsand that he is writing lyrics 'with more music and painting than before, so as to get people to hear and see'. This remark could apply to a number of poems in *MW*, where evidence for precise dating is lacking, including 'Fra Lippo Lippi', 'A Toccata of Galuppi's', 'Master Hugues of Saxe-Gotha', and 'Old Pictures in Florence'.

This has been 'a very happy winter', EBB writes to Jameson, 'with nothing from without to vex us much'. RB and EBB have been 'meditating Socialism and mysticism of very various kinds, deep in Louis Blanc and Proudhon, deeper in the German spiritualists'. She also continues to read French novels and to take an interest in 'my rapping spirits, of whom our American guests bring us relays of witnesses'. Recommending French poetry to MRM this month she mentions Musset ('best to my mind when he is most lyrical') and Edgar Quinet's *Ahasuérus* (1833).

March

15   (Tues) EBB is busy with 'a new poem' (*AL*) and revisions for a third edition (1854) of *Poems*. RB is also 'busy with another book' (*MW*). Recently he has read Dumas *fils*' 'Diane de Lys' ('clever – only outrageous as to the morals').

17   He may begin 'Andrea del Sarto' (*MW*) soon after this date, on which he replies to John Kenyon's letter asking

him to obtain a copy of what at this time is thought to be a portrait of Andrea and his Lucrezia in the Pitti Palace. RB explains that the cost of such a copy would be prohibitive; in November 1881 he will tell F.J. Furnivall that he sent Kenyon the poem instead. At about the same time he probably writes 'Old Pictures in Florence'.

April

6   (Wed) RB sends EBB's revisions for the first volume of her *Poems* (1854) to Chapman. On 15 he sends the new preliminary speech for Lucifer in 'A Drama of Exile'.

12   RB is reading Bulwer-Lytton's *My Novel* (1853).

13   EBB notes that RB is 'fond of digging at Vasari'. He may well be working at this time on one or other of his Vasari-connected poems for *MW*, 'Fra Lippo Lippi', 'Andrea del Sarto', and 'Old Pictures in Florence'; but he has long been a keen reader of Vasari.

16   RB's *Colombe's Birthday* is performed at the Haymarket Theatre; six more performances follow. In giving (renewed) permission to Helena Faucit Martin, who plays Colombe, to put on the play, he stipulates only that the corrections in the 1849 text should be followed. He allows the play to be cut to three acts.

Late this month EBB reads and is favourably impressed by Matthew Arnold's *Empedocles on Etna, and Other Poems* (1852). RB also reads 'Empedocles', which almost certainly influences his 'Cleon' (*MW*), written probably at some point between now and early 1854.

May

c. 1   (Sun) EBB tells Arabel that RB now has nearly enough lyrics for a volume.

June

Early in the month Helena Faucit Martin's production of *Colombe* is repeated in Manchester.

July

13   (Wed) In the evening EBB and RB are entertained, at the Bellosguardo villa of the diplomat and writer

Robert Lytton (son of Edward Bulwer-Lytton), with strawberries and cream and much talk of spiritualism with EBB's fellow enthusiasts Frederick Tennyson (AT's brother), Hiram Powers, and Professor Pasquale Villari. RB remains sceptical.

15   The family goes to Bagni di Lucca, staying at Casa Tolomei, La Villa, at a cost of about £11 for thirteen weeks. Here they become intimate with the sculptor and writer William Wetmore Story (1819–95) and his family, who are staying at the Bagni Caldi. EBB continues to work on *AL*. RB continues, in his 'cheerful little blue room with two windows', to work on *MW*. One piece known to date from this time is 'In a Balcony'. 'Up at a Villa – Down in the City' may also be written here.

August

20   (Sat) or 21 The Brownings and Storys visit Benabbia and the surrounding mountains; writing to MRM on 21 EBB contrasts the lanes, meadowland, and great trees of England with the jagged mountains 'setting their teeth against the sky!'; 'You may as well guess at a lion by a lady's lapdog, as at nature by what you see in England'. Cp. *AL*, I. 615–45.

September

c. 15   (Thurs) The Brownings and Storys go on an expedition into the hills, to Prato Fiorito. The scenery clearly informs RB's 'By the Fireside' (*MW*), probably written at about this time, but some elements derive from his reading for a planned trip to Lake Orta in early 1847.

About now EBB reads (and approves of) Charlotte Brontë's *Villette* and Elizabeth Gaskell's *Ruth*.

October

10   (Mon) They return to Florence. The time at Bagni di Lucca has been happy and 'not idle either'. RB especially has done a considerable amount of work and is determined to have *MW* ready by the spring. *AL* is

growing and will be longer than AT's *The Princess*; she
means it to be 'unquestionably her best work'.

15   EBB's *Poems*, 3rd edition, is published by Chapman &
     Hall at 16s. Revisions include the new opening lines of
     'A Drama of Exile'.

At about mid-month the Brownings see Verdi's 'very pas-
sionate and dramatic' *Il Trovatore* at the Pergola.

November

15   (Tues) The Brownings leave for Rome, visiting Perugia,
     Assisi, and Terni. Arriving in Rome on 22, they rent
     rooms on the third floor of 43 Via Bocca di Leone.

23   Joe Story, six-year-old son of the Storys, dies of gastric
     fever. EBB and RB spend most of the day at his
     bedside. EBB in particular is terrified that Pen will
     catch the fever, from which Joe's sister Edith and
     another child recover. Soon afterwards EBB visits, with
     Emelyn Story, the child's grave in the Protestant
     Cemetery.

December

Thackeray and his daughters call on the Brownings. They
meet again a number of times early in 1854. The sixteen-
year-old Anne Thackeray (later Ritchie) finds EBB 'the
greatest woman I ever knew in my life ... She has white
teeth and a low harsh voice, her eyes are bright and full of
life ... She is great upon mysticism and listens with a
solemn eager manner to any nonsense people like to tell
her upon that subject'. Later she will note that EBB seemed
'to carry her own atmosphere always, something serious,
motherly, absolutely artless, and yet impassioned, noble,
and sincere'.

1854

January

9   (Mon) EBB and RB visit the Colosseum.

Among their main friends in Rome at this time are Fanny
Kemble and her sister Adelaide Sartoris and, by the spring,

the young sculptor Harriet (Hatty) Hosmer (1830–1908), who is of particular interest to EBB, writing *AL*, as one who 'emancipates the eccentric life of a perfectly "emancipated female" from all shadow of blame by the purity of hers' (to MRM, 10 May).

February
16 (Thurs) RB's *Colombe's Birthday* is performed at the Athenaeum, Boston.
In mid–late February he unexpectedly meets Monclar, his friend of twenty years ago, on the Pincio.
28 The Brownings and the Prince of Prussia attend a musical evening at the home of the archaeologist August Emil Braun and his wife Anne, formerly Anne Thomson (see April 1845).

March
 3 (Fri) RB, with Adelaide and Edward Sartoris, Robert Lytton, John Gibson Lockhart, and others, goes on a three-carriage excursion to the coast. During or after this trip Lockhart makes the remark (often quoted by EBB and RB) 'I like Browning – he isn't at all like a damned literary man'. RB takes part in at least three more such expeditions this month, going to 'Valderano' (probably Valleranello) *c*. 15, Ostia *c*. 22, and Frascati *c*. 28–30.
20 By this date EBB has written 'A Plea for the Ragged Schools of London', responding to her sister Arabel's request for poems by her and RB which can be sold at a bazaar in Baker Street, on 19 April, in aid of the Ragged Schools.
Edith Story is gravely ill once more. Her parents set off for Naples, considered much healthier than Rome, but from Velletri, on 23 or 24, Story sends a desperate note to RB asking him to join them at what appears to be Edith's deathbed. She recovers, however, and he is able to return the following day.
30 By now he has completed his offering for Arabel's bazaar, 'The Twins' (reprinted in *MW*).

Between March and May RB sits for his portrait by the American artist William Page, who lives beneath the Brownings with his younger wife Sarah. During composition of 'Andrea del Sarto' (*MW*) RB is probably influenced by Sarah's affair with a Neapolitan nobleman, her relationship with her husband, and Page's theory that Titian originally painted in subdued tones – as he, 'The American Titian' therefore also does (see Markus, pp. 197–206).

April

19 (Wed) By this date Chapman & Hall have printed, at the Brownings' expense, several hundred copies (price 6d.) of *Two Poems by Elizabeth Barrett and Robert Browning* (see 20 and 30 March). Sales are poor.

27 RB has finished 'Ben Karshook's Wisdom' at the request of Bryan Waller Procter to help the impoverished Marguerite A. Power (niece of the Countess of Blessington), editor of the annual *The Keepsake*. EBB provides 'My Kate' (*LP*) earlier in April and it is included at the end of 1854 in the Keepsake for 1855; 'Ben Karshook' appears late in 1855 in the 1856 number.

The weather is warm enough in Rome for EBB to join 'pic nic' excursions in the Campagna organised by Fanny Kemble and Adelaide Sartoris where the talk is 'almost too brilliant for the sentiment of the scenery'. (Among the places visited are Castel Fusano and Villa Adriana.) Clearly RB's 'Two in the Campagna' (*MW*) arises partly from such expeditions and is perhaps written in May or June. The Campagna is also one inspiration for his 'Love Among the Ruins' (*MW*). (The subject-matter of the *MW* poems 'Protus' and 'Holy-Cross Day' possibly – but not necessarily – suggests that they too were written in Rome in 1853–4.)

May

25 (Thurs) Charles Hemans presents his mother Felicia's Commonplace Book to EBB.

28 The family leaves Rome.

June

c. 2   (Fri) They reach Florence. RB probably finishes here, having begun in Rome, 'An Epistle Containing the Strange Medical Experience of Karshish, the Arab Physician' (*MW*). Soon after the return to Florence, Flush dies aged thirteen. This summer the Brownings stay in the city because of lack of funds; the *David Lyon* has provided nothing and Kenyon forgets to send his six-monthly £50. The books are earning little. A hundred copies of *CGW* are still unsold.

September

EBB is worried to hear that her father has fallen and broken his leg. She has Penini address a letter to him in the hope that he will at least open it. The result is unknown.

Financial problems are alleviated when EBB learns that the *David Lyon* will soon yield her a dividend of £175.

December

8   The papal bull *Ineffabilis Deus* proclaims the Immaculate Conception, which is referred to in 'Bishop Blougram's Apology' (*MW*), line 704. The poem, which also in line 938 refers to 'this [Crimean] war' of March 1854 onwards, probably dates at least in part from 1854–5.

1855

January

By 10 (Wed) EBB has written 4500 lines of *AL*.

10   Death of MRM.

For much of the month EBB suffers from her 'old illness' mainly in the form of a racking cough. RB and Wilson minister to her and the pain is relieved with the aid of coffee and morphine.

February

24   (Sat) EBB, writing to Anna Jameson, argues that Florence Nightingale's professionalisation of nursing is unhelpful to the cause of women; men are happy to

bend the knee before nurses' traditional female virtues but 'if they stir an inch as thinkers or artists from the beaten line ... the very same men would curse the impudence of the very same women'.

March

6 (Tues) EBB tells Eliza Ogilvy that she is 'not nearly at an end of the composition even' of *AL* while RB 'has at least all his rough work done' for *MW*. By 20 April he is dictating for four hours a day to Isa Blagden, increasingly the Brownings' closest friend in Florence. Later each day EBB criticises the results. Some time this spring EBB, Hatty Hosmer, and Elizabeth Kinney (1810–89) disguise themselves as boys or young men with the intention of going to see some paintings somewhere in Florence where 'no woman was ever admitted within the gates'. (RB and William Burnet Kinney will appear to be their tutors.) As they prepare to set off, according to Elizabeth Kinney, excitement gives EBB's 'usually pale face a fine colour, and her large black eyes an unwonted brightness'. In this excitement (perhaps opium-induced, says Kinney), EBB goes into the street; the other women go after her to bring her back and, in their unlikely disguises, all three begin to attract unwanted attention. EBB begins to cry and RB, 'as pale as death with fright', insists on calling off the whole escapade.

June

12 (Tues) Elizabeth Wilson marries, in an Anglican service at the British Embassy, her fellow employee at Casa Guidi, Ferdinando Romagnoli. Unknown to their employers, she is four months pregnant by him. (See also 10 July.)

13 The Brownings, with Wilson and Romagnoli, leave Florence. Having missed the boat from Livorno they spend the night in Pisa before returning to Florence on 14. On 20 they sail successfully from Livorno for Corsica and Marseille and arrive in Paris on 24 (138 Avenue des

Champs-Elysées). In Marseille they meet, by chance, EBB's brother Alfred, who on 1 August in Paris will marry his cousin Lizzie Barrett and be disinherited by his father. More immediately Alfred is responsible for recovering lost luggage for the Brownings.

RB has been 'frantic about the Crimea', EBB tells SB on 15; mismanagement of the war is the consequence of the British class system. If reform results 'more good will have been done by this one great shock to the heart of England than by fifty years' more patching, pottering, and knocking impotent heads together'. EBB largely agrees with this and is particularly delighted by the contrastingly good organisation of the French army in the Crimea.

July

In Paris in late June or early July the Brownings attend a reception given by Mary Mohl at which Prosper Mérimée, the historian François-Auguste Mignet, the philosopher Victor Cousin, and the actress Adelaide Ristori (see 10 April 1856) are also present.

10   (Tues) After difficulties attendant on a Catholic/ Protestant marriage have been resolved, the church wedding of Wilson and Romagnoli takes place. (A Roman Catholic wedding and vows are necessary for the marriage to become legal in Tuscany).

11–12   The family travels from Paris to an apartment at 13, Dorset Street, London. On 12 they are visited by Adelaide Sartoris and on 14 breakfast with Kenyon to meet 'half America and a quarter of London'.

23   At the house of Mr and Mrs Rymer of Ealing EBB and RB meet the American medium Daniel Dunglas Home, the principal inspiration for RB's 'Mr Sludge, the Medium' (*DP*). Various 'manifestations' occur, and a spirit hand appears to place a wreath of clematis on EBB's head. She is convinced of the genuineness of these phenomena while RB is convinced that trickery is involved. His hosts will not allow him to pursue his investigations or to attend another séance. When (on

about 25) Home and Mrs Rymer call at Dorset Street he expresses his contempt for the medium. The extent of the difference of opinion between RB and EBB on spiritualism has become apparent; she asks several of her correspondents not to mention the subject in their letters.

In July or early August friends seen in London include Ruskin (14 and 24 July), Carlyle, Forster, Procter, Kemble, and A.W. Kinglake.

August
Towards the end of the month Elizabeth Wilson reveals that she is pregnant. EBB is for a time 'shocked and pained' and anxious for Pen.

31 (Fri) Mr Barrett sends those of the family who still live at Wimpole Street to Eastbourne. In mid-August he had seen Pen playing at Wimpole Street with George Barrett, asked 'Whose child is that, George?' and, told 'Ba's child', simply said 'And what is he doing here, pray?' and changed the subject.

September
22 (Sat) RB, very close to finishing work on the proofs of *MW*, which has occupied him and EBB for much of their time in London, writes the fair copy of the concluding 'One Word More', evidently composed soon before.

23 Milsand, writing to W.H. Darley about the first volume (in proof) of *MW*, which he received on 10 August, makes the first known use of the term 'dramatic monologue'. His article on the work, including translations from many poems, will appear in the *Revue contemporaine* on 15 September 1856.

26 and 27 AT and Dante Gabriel Rossetti dine with the Brownings at Dorset Street. On 27 AT reads *Maud*, and RB *Fra Lippo Lippi*, to a group also including SB, Arabel, Ford Madox Brown, William Michael Rossetti and William Holman Hunt. EBB is captivated by AT's 'frankness, confidingness, and unexampled *naïveté*'. He reads

'exquisitely in a voice like an organ, rather music than
speech', while RB reads 'with as much sprightly varia-
tion as there was in Tennyson of sustained continuity'.

October

Early in the month the Brownings dine with Ruskin,
Adelaide Sartoris, and Frederick Leighton.

3   (Thurs) By now printing of the two volumes of *MW* is
    complete. Wilson goes to her sister's house, where
    Orestes Wilson Romagnoli is born on 13.

By 16 Dante Gabriel Rossetti finishes his portrait of RB.

17 The Brownings depart for Paris, renting at 102 Rue de
    Grenelle, for £2 a week, a too-small apartment whose
    yellow sofas they particularly dislike. The apartment
    has been found for them by their friends the Corkrans.
    As usual in Paris, EBB particularly enjoys looking in
    shop windows. (The description of the city's streets in
    AL 6.79ff. is written by early March 1856.)

In the last week of the month the Brownings are visited by
Sir Edward Bulwer-Lytton and Robert Lytton; RB listens
patiently to the elder Lytton's defence of Home's veracity
while the younger quietly gives EBB a more extravagant
account of Home's flying about in T.A. Trollope's house in
Florence.

November

10 (Sat) RB's *Men and Women* is published in two volumes
    by Chapman & Hall at 12s.

17 A largely unfavourable review of *MW* in *The
    Athenaeum* begins a series of responses bitterly disap-
    pointing to RB and EBB. (There are more positive
    responses from Rossetti, Carlyle, and George Eliot
    who, in the *Westminster Review* in January 1856,
    admires the poet's 'robust energy ... informed by a
    subtle, penetrating spirit'.)

Dante Gabriel Rossetti comes to Paris, goes to the Louvre
with RB, and notes his remarkably extensive knowledge of
early Italian art.

December

2 (Sun) Ruskin sends RB a detailed letter expressing his puzzlement with much in *MW*. This elicits RB's reply of 10, including the statement that poetry puts 'the infinite within the finite'.

8 The American edition of *MW*, in one volume, is published by Ticknor & Fields, Boston, who pay RB £60.

13 The Brownings move to more satisfactory accommodation at 3 Rue du Colisée, where EBB is at last able to resume work on *AL* for the first time since leaving Florence in June. At the end of the month she begins to transcribe finished parts of the poem from the rough drafts.

1856

EBB's 'A Curse for a Nation' is published in *The Liberty Bell*, Boston. (Another version will appear in *PBC*.)

January

Ruskin presents RB with a copy of his *Modern Painters*, Volume III.

30 (Wed) RB has read and is enthusiastic about the second book of *AL*. He finishes the third book on 5 February, the fourth on 14, the fifth on 27, the sixth on 13 March.

February

Ruskin's notable praise and extensive quotation of RB's 'The Bishop Orders his Tomb' appears in *Modern Painters*, Volume IV. 'Nobody', RB laments to his often dilatory publisher Chapman in April, 'will snip that round into a neat little paragraph, and head it "Ruskin on Browning", and stick it among the "News of the Week", "Topics of the Day", as the friendly method is'.

In February–March RB works on, but abandons, a revision of *Sordello*. (Some of the revisions in *1863*, however, may date from this period.)

March–April
EBB writes the seventh and eighth books of *AL*.

April
10 (Thurs) RB spends an evening with Dickens and Macready at the former's apartment in the Avenue des Champs-Elysées. Probably all three have just seen Adelaide Ristori in Legouvé's *Médée*, which opened in Paris on 8. Dickens and Macready dislike her acting. RB's opinion is more moderate – having seen this and another Ristori production he thinks 'the Médée very fine' but 'won't join in the cry about miraculous genius and Rachel out-Racheled' (EBB to Anna Jameson, 2 May).

c. 18–20 Chapman proposes a new edition of EBB's *Poems*, to include *CGW*.

RB is busy with social life (dining on one occasion with Milnes, Sand, Mignet, and the future architect of Italian unification Cavour) and drawing; EBB tells Jameson on 2 May that 'after thirteen days' application he has produced some quite startling copies of heads' and that he cannot, like her, 'rest from serious work in light literature'.

May
12 (Mon) EBB sends Chapman proofs of the first volume of *Poems*, 1856. The second and third (*CGW*) follow on 26.
23 RB asks Chapman to send him as soon as possible William Berry's *Genealogica Sacra: or, Scripture Tables, Compiled from the Holy Bible* (1819).

June
EBB completes the ninth and final book of *AL*.
14 (Sat) RB watches the baptism of Napoleon III's son the Prince Imperial at Notre-Dame and afterwards, according to 'Apparent Failure' (*DP*), goes to the Morgue.
29 The family travels to London. John Kenyon, in his final illness on the Isle of Wight, lends them his house in London at 39 Devonshire Place.

Either this summer or in 1858 the bookseller Thomas Hookham shows RB letters from Harriet, Shelley's first wife, which considerably shake his faith in the 'Sun Treader'. He had believed that she was uneducated and that the couple parted by mutual consent.

July
Wilson re-enters the Brownings' service, leaving her son Orestes with her family.

9 (Wed) RB records that he has finished 'this divine Book', meaning specifically the seventh book rather than *AL* as a whole. EBB is feeling 'overpowered' with work and is kept going only by her morphine.

13 RB and EBB meet Nathaniel Hawthorne at one of Milnes' breakfast parties.

August
9 (Sat) By this date the manuscript of *AL* has been sent to the printers.

23 The Brownings move to Ventnor on the Isle of Wight, whither, soon after their arrival in England, Mr Barrett has sent Arabel and those of her brothers still living at Wimpole Street. RB and EBB work on proofs of *AL*, sent after them in a steady stream from London.

September
6 (Sat) – 22 The Brownings stay with Kenyon at 3 Parade, West Cowes, Isle of Wight. Proofs of *AL* continue to follow them. Arabel and George Barrett are also involved, reading revises in Ventnor.

22–30 Visit to Henrietta Cook and her family in Taunton.

30 The family returns to London.

October
10 (Fri) The fog and mist of London are affecting EBB so badly that RB is 'at my wits end to imagine how to get her through the long journey that lies before us'. (In the event she will recover rapidly during the journey.) He is also worried about money and wants to know at

once from Reuben Browning 'what my actual means
are before I set out'.

17   EBB dates her dedication to Kenyon of *AL*, 'the most
mature of my works, and the one into which my
highest convictions upon Life and Art have entered'.

18   On or shortly before this date she is sent by Coventry
Patmore, to her anger and incredulity, his article
including remarks on 'the privilege of [women's] sub-
ordination to men' in *The National Review* for October.
If Patmore is to be consistent, she fears (wrongly as it
turns out), his review of *AL* for *The North British Review*
(February 1857) must be entirely hostile.

23   Having finished work on the last revises of *AL*, EBB
and RB leave London. They stop briefly in Paris, meet
Joseph Milsand briefly at the station in Dijon, arrive in
Marseille on 26 and sail from there for Genoa and
Livorno on 28. They reach Casa Guidi on 30.

November

1   (Sat) EBB's *Poems*, 'fourth edition' (price 18s.), is published by Chapman & Hall. Newly included are *CGW*
and three poems of 1845–6, 'A Denial', 'Proof and
Disproof', and 'Question and Answer'. The work is
reprinted as the 'fifth edition' in 1862.

15   EBB's *Aurora Leigh* is published by Chapman & Hall
at 12s. and by C.S. Francis of New York at $1. Francis,
who pirated earlier works by EBB, this time pays
£100 for the right to publish on the same day as
Chapman.

AL sells rapidly and attracts enthusiastic responses from
Ruskin, Leigh Hunt, the Rossettis and many others.
Published reviews mix praise with puzzlement at or
disdain for the poem's length, earnestness, or 'fantastic
images'.

December

3   (Wed) Death of John Kenyon at West Cowes. He leaves
EBB £4500 and RB £6500, investment of which will give
them £700 a year and financial security. Since the

money is not payable for a year, however – and there is no Kenyon to send his annual £100 – they continue to have short-term money worries.

26 EBB has sent for a library copy of *Jane Eyre* to check how closely Rochester's loss of sight there resembles Romney's in *AL*. (She points up the differences, from memory, in a letter of this date to Anna Jameson.)

1857

January

At the end of the month a second impression of *AL* is published by Chapman & Hall. EBB tells Jameson on 2 February that she wishes she deserved all the praise given her for the poem; 'I see too distinctly what I *ought* to have written. Still, it is nearer the mark than my former efforts – fuller, stronger, more sustained'.

February

Late this month, during carnival, EBB (usually not well enough for such occasions) accompanies RB, in domino and mask, to the 'great opera ball'.

March

Late this month a third impression of *AL* is published by Chapman & Hall.

April

8 (Wed) Harriet Beecher Stowe calls at Casa Guidi. EBB is affected less by her books than by the fact that she has moved the world further than all her contemporaries, male or female, in the direction of good. (EBB first expressed enthusiasm for *Uncle Tom's Cabin* and for the abolitionist cause in America in a letter to Jameson of 12 April 1853.) At this time the Brownings are reading Victor Hugo's *Les Contemplations* (1856), which inspires her to draft a letter – not sent – to Napoleon III, appealing to him to forgive his enemy Hugo and recall him from exile.

17   Death of EBB's father Edward Moulton-Barrett. She is left with a feeling of 'sudden desolation'. She takes some comfort from Julia Martin's news, a little before Barrett's death, that in response to her plea for him to forgive his married children he had written to say that he had forgiven them and prayed for them and their families. The eldest surviving son, Charles John (Stormie), makes over £5000 of the inheritance to each of the children disowned by their father – EBB, Henrietta and Alfred.

June
EBB is teaching Pen German.

July
30   (Thurs) The Brownings go again to Bagni di Lucca, renting Casa Betti, La Villa.

August
1   (Sat) EBB sends her 'Amy's Cruelty' for inclusion in Marguerite A. Power's *Keepsake*.
c. 2   Friends including Isa Blagden and Robert Lytton stay at the Albergo Pelicano (until early September). Lytton, already ill on arrival, is nursed through severe gastric fever by Blagden and RB.
29   Wilson, about six months pregnant, is taken ill and goes back to Florence. Her replacement, Annunziata, is also ill for a few days. Wilson now leaves the Brownings' employment permanently, but continues useful to them in Florence by, for instance, looking after the aged and awkward W.S. Landor (see October 1859). Her husband Ferdinando Romagnoli continues to work at Casa Guidi until 1861.

September
Probably at the beginning of this month the Brownings and their new friends Sophie and David Eckley stay briefly at Gallicano. RB, on a mountain ride with David Eckley, saves himself by clinging to a crag when his horse trips and falls sixty feet.

c. 18   (Fri) Pen develops gastric fever but recovers by the end of the month.

October
5   (Mon) RB identifies a manuscript shown him by Clotilda Stisted, a well known social figure in the expatriate community of Bagni di Lucca, as that of Shelley's 'Indian Serenade', found on his body. He sends it to Leigh Hunt.
7   The Brownings return to Florence, where EBB's friendship with Sophie Eckley continues close. Both she and her husband David are devoted to the Brownings; RB is somewhat suspicious of Sophie, who clearly knows how to keep EBB happy with descriptions of her contact with the spirits.

This Autumn EBB and RB read Flaubert's *Madame Bovary*, which Pen will describe as 'Papa's favourite book' in January 1859.

1858

January
9   (Sat) 'The celebrated Improvisatrice … the Signorina Milli' visits EBB and RB. Anna Jameson is also present.

April
At about the beginning of this month RB buys a skeleton. EBB prefers not to look at it.
12   (Mon) She tells Arabel that she is still feeling weak and struggling against habitual sadness at the loss of their father nearly a year before.

June
8   (Tues) Nathaniel and Sophia Hawthorne, the Eckleys, Fanny Haworth, and the American poet William Cullen Bryant, spend the evening at Casa Guidi. They talk about spiritualism. Hawthorne finds RB cordial, informative, and surprisingly clear in conversation considering how difficult his poetry is, and EBB kind,

remarkably small, 'scarcely embodied at all'; she and Pen are of elfin breed and quite likely to flit away.

26   RB is at Isa Blagden's villa with Hawthorne, T.A. Trollope, and the American composer Francis Boott. Hawthorne notes that even Browning's nonsense is excellent, 'the true bubble and effervescence of a bright and powerful mind'. Given the opportunity, he would like the poet much and would make the feeling mutual.

At the end of the month Sophie Eckley showers EBB with gifts on the eve of her departure for France.

July

1   (Thurs) The Brownings set off for Paris. They sail from Livorno to Genoa (spending the night on the deck of the crowded boat) and Marseille, where they stay at Hôtel du Louvre on 3. They go on by express trains, spending nights at Hotel Côlet, Lyon (4) and Hôtel du Parc, Dijon (5).

6   They arrive in Paris and stay at the Hôtel Hyacinthe. They see Anna Jameson during the first few days here, and then Father Prout (see November 1848). They visit, and RB helps to feed, Lady Elgin, who has just had the latest in a series of strokes.

19   They leave Paris. They rent a 'hideous' house at Le Havre (2 Rue de Perry). RB Senior and SB live in part of the house and Arabel and George Barrett come to stay, as for a time do Henry Barrett and his wife (since 21 April) Amelia, and Joseph Milsand. EBB finds the mixed company exhausting. RB also finds the time here unsatisfying.

September

18   (Sat) She is photographed in Le Havre by Cyrus Macaire. On 19 RB suggests to Chapman that an engraving from the photograph should appear in the proposed revised edition of *AL*. (The engraving is eventually undertaken in November, with D.G. and W.M. Rossetti supervising the work.)

20   The Brownings return to Paris (accompanied for a time by Arabel), to an apartment at 6 Rue Castiglione. Visitors here include Thackeray and his daughters.

October

5   (Tues) EBB is angry about Dickens' open letter of 25 May on his separation from his wife. He is using 'his genius as a cudgel against his near kin', 'taking advantage of his hold with the public to turn public opinion against her'.

18   The Brownings leave Paris, travelling by Mâcon, Chambéry (19–21; here they visit Rousseau's house Les Charmettes, where RB plays the harpsichord), Lanslebourg and Mont Cenis, Susa (22), Turin (23), and a stormy eighteen-hour passage from Genoa to Livorno (24–25). They arrive in Florence on 26, soon after which EBB begins revising *AL*.

November

19   (Fri) Still seeking a warmer climate for EBB, the Brownings set off with the Eckleys, in their two carriages, for Rome. They sleep at Poggio Bagnoli on 19, Camuscia (having passed through Arezzo) on 20, Perugia on 21 and Spoleto on 22. On 23 RB, with David Eckley and his mother-in-law, goes to the Falls of Terni; having spent the remaining two nights at Terni and Civita Castellana they reach Rome on the afternoon of 25. (During the journey RB succeeds in breaking up a dangerous fight between two drivers of oxen-teams.) On 26 they again rent 43 Via Bocca di Leone at £11 a month. EBB is unable to go out for several weeks while RB, as usual, enjoys an active social life. He models in clay under Story's instruction.

December

25   (Sat) The Brownings and the Eckleys attend the Christmas 'Grand Mass' at St Peter's.

1859

January
1 (Sat) By this date EBB has sent to Chapman the corrected first seven books of *AL*; the remaining two books follow on 14 or 15.

RB is in good health and spirits. He walks every morning with David Eckley at 6 o'clock. He has been out every evening for a fortnight 'and sometimes two or three times deep in a one night's engagements. So plenty of distraction, and no Men and Women' (EBB to Blagden, 7 January). When he goes out EBB goes to bed and reads books including the works of Swedenborg. Among the many friends and acquaintances seen by RB and, less often, by EBB, are the young artist Frederick Leighton, Charlotte Cushman, the Storys, the Hawthornes, and William Page. RB draws twice a week under the supervision of Emma Landseer Mackenzie of Via Pedacchia. By 7 he has seen three theatre productions starring Adelaide Ristori.

12 He probably goes to at least part of the Storys' grand ball at Palazzo Barberini.

26 Treaty of Turin: Napoleon III enters an alliance with Sardinia/Piedmont.

This month RB calls on Louisa Crawford to indicate his anger at the attacks, in her sister Julia Ward Howe's *Words for the Hour* (1858), on EBB. (Howe claims, for instance, that her 'unearthly' verse is inspired by some 'nameless draught ... a drug'. With reference to this remark EBB acknowledges to Eckley that only morphine has kept her alive.)

February
6 (Sun) RB hears the future Cardinal Manning preach 'the poorest, most illogical, most impudent of sermons'.

In the first half of the month EBB is reading John Lothrop Motley's *The Rise of the Dutch Republic* (1856) and finding it a little dull. RB reads the first volume of Carlyle's *History of*

Frederick II of Prussia (1858–65) and 'curses and swears over' it; EBB finds it 'immoral ... in the brutal sense' (to Blagden, 15 February).

March

Early in the month Field Talfourd draws EBB in charcoal. An engraving from his drawing will be included in the new *AL* edition, on proof corrections for which EBB is now working. She sends the last of them to Chapman on 19. Massimo d'Azeglio, Piedmontese ambassador in Rome and former prime minister, visits Via Bocca di Leone and expresses himself 'full of hope for Italy'.

18 (Fri) RB dines with the Prince of Wales and tells him about the Italian political situation.

26 RB visits Ostia and Castel Fusano.

April

23 (Sat) Austria attacks Sardinia/Piedmont; France declares war on Austria on 3 May.

27 The Brownings and Eckleys visit Tivoli.

May

RB is confident that he hears 'the prime of the news' of the war and political situation because he knows 'the really instructed people' in Rome: the diplomat Odo Russell, the former ambassador in Constantinople Lord Stratford de Redcliffe, Henry Wreford of *The Times*.

9 (Mon) EBB is sitting for a portrait by Frederick Lehmann, completed on 15. By 22 he has completed a portrait of RB.

26 The Brownings leave Rome and have reached Siena, where they spend the night at Hotel Algride, by 29. They arrive in Florence on 30. Elizabeth Wilson, who now runs a lodging-house, comes to greet them; when they speak alone, EBB discovers that Wilson is suffering from religious mania and delusions – the world is about to end, her sons are fruits of the first resurrection, an angel has carried Orestes through the air.

To EBB's particular joy the Grand Duke has fled, French troops are in Florence, and the end of Austrian domination seems imminent.

June

4   (Sat) The French and Piedmontese defeat the Austrians at Magenta. On 8 the French general, MacMahon, rescues a child in danger of being crushed during the victorious entry to Milan. EBB uses this incident in 'Napoleon III in Italy' (*PBC*; ll. 242 ff.).

11   The revised (so-called 'fourth') edition of *AL* is published by Chapman & Hall.

24   the French and Piedmontese are again victorious at Solferino, but heavy French losses are among the factors which precipitate the Treaty of Villafranca (see 11 July).

July

RB takes charge of the irascible Walter Savage Landor, expelled by his wife from their house in Fiesole. By arrangement with John Forster and Landor's brothers he becomes official guardian.

11   (Mon) At Villafranca (following an armistice on 8) France makes peace with Austria. Lombardy will be united with Piedmont but other parts of northern Italy are to remain under Austrian control. Disappointment at this unexpected outcome contributes to a collapse of EBB's now fragile health; 'lungs and heart were out of order together it seemed', she will tell Eliza Ogilvy at the end of October. She is in bed for nearly three weeks. Hearing of Villafranca she fell 'from the mountains of the moon where I had walked hand in hand with a beautiful dream'. Only briefly, however, does she lose faith in Napoleon III against the powers – Britain, above all – which she perceives as baulking his plans to aid Italy.

After Villafranca RB destroys his poem on 'the Italian question' (possibly an early version of *Prince Hohenstiel*) since 'it no longer suited the moment', while EBB decides to stand by her 'Napoleon III in Italy', which is already written or in progress. They had intended to publish the two poems together.

18 RB delivers Landor to the Storys in Siena.

30 Advised by Dr E.G.T. Grisanowsky to seek a change of air for EBB, the Brownings go to Siena, staying at first at the Hotel Algride.

August

1 (Mon) They move to Villa Alberti, Marciano. The Storys are established nearby, with Landor, at Villa Belvedere. EBB, so weak that she has to be carried on and off the train and to bed at the hotel, is ill and exhausted for the first ten days or so. She recovers sufficiently to work on 'A Tale of Villafranca', 'An August Voice', and other *PBC* poems.

Probably in late August or September EBB sends Sophie Eckley a letter from Siena which, tactfully expressing some doubts about the authenticity of some of the spiritualist experiences they have had together, marks the beginning of the end of their close friendship. Eckley appears to have deceived her by fabricating spiritualist experiences for her benefit. EBB's 'Where's Agnes?' (*LP*), clearly inspired by her disenchantment with Eckley, is written about now, or perhaps in Rome in 1860.

September

2 (Fri) Odo Russell visits the Brownings in Siena on his way to Rome. Isa Blagden and Kate Field come to stay.

24 EBB's 'A Tale of Villafranca' (*PBC*), written in Siena, is published in *The Athenaeum*. She sent it to H.F. Chorley on 12, asking him to publish it 'in spite of its good and true politics, which you "Athenaeum" people (being English) will dissent from altogether'. Later, in October, she sends 'to your private ear' what becomes in *PBC* the seventh stanza ('A great Deed in this world of ours? ...') which she suspects would have led to the poem's rejection.

Pen is bought the pony which he has been riding.

October

9   (Sun) EBB feels strong enough to go to see 'the divine Eve of Sodoma' but is prevented or deterred from entering the cathedral by its steps.

10   Return to Florence.

RB arranges for Landor to be taken in (from 6 November) by Elizabeth Wilson, whose religious mania now seems less acute. She opens a larger lodging-house in Via Nunziatina (subsequently Via della Chiesa) and is paid £30 a year by Landor's family in England.

November

EBB and RB read Chorley's novel *Roccabella*, which depicts proponents of the Risorgimento unfavourably. It is dedicated, sarcastically they suspect, to EBB. On 25 (Fri) she acknowledges the dedication and defends her belief in Italy and 'our sublime Azeglios and acute Cavours and energetic Farinis'.

28   They set off from Florence for Rome, spending nights at Poggio Imperiale (28), Passignano (29), Foligno (30) and Terni (31), after which their route is uncertain. On 28 and 29 RB reads Victor Hugo's *La Légende des siècles* (1859), given EBB by Isa Blagden just before they leave.

December

3   (Sat) They arrive in Rome, where, after a night at the Hotel d'Angleterre, they rent a large apartment at 28 Via del Tritone for only £11 a month. (There is a dearth of visitors because of fears of impending war.)

During the winter of 1859–60 they know the American Unitarian minister Theodore Parker, whose ideas on evolving human conceptions of deity may well have influenced RB to write 'Caliban Upon Setebos' (*DP*) at about this time. (Darwin's *Origin of Species*, published on 24 November, is another likely influence, in part mediated through Parker.)

1860

January
EBB sees Sophie Eckley several times this winter, but their old intimacy is over.

At about mid-month RB and EBB go to see a display of swords designed by the jeweller Castellani for presentation to Napoleon III and Victor Emanuel. At Castellani's they are made much of and asked for autographs. After this outing EBB suffers for some days from breathlessness, irregular heart-beat, and persistent coughing.

c. 28   (Sat) RB receives copies of an 1858 edition of Paolo Sarpi's *History of the Council of Trent* (1619) and an *Orlando Furioso* of 1854, which he has asked Blagden to obtain for him in Florence.

EBB writes or finishes work on two *PBC* poems, 'The Dance' and 'A Court Lady'. Proofs of all the other poems in *PBC* have arrived back from Chapman by the end of the month.

February
6   (Mon) EBB sends to Chapman the preface to *PBC*, probably soon after it is written. Its bold attack on British attitudes ('non-intervention in the affairs of neighbouring states is a high political virtue; but non-intervention does not mean, passing by on the other side when your neighbour falls among thieves') makes the collection all the more controversial at home.

The Brownings see Harriet Beecher Stowe again.

March
11   (Sun) A plebiscite of males over twenty-one makes Tuscany part of Victor Emanuel's kingdom.

12   EBB's *Poems before Congress* is published by Chapman & Hall at 4s. The title refers to an expected congress on Italy which failed to take place in January. (C.S. Francis pirates the work in New York as *Napoleon III in Italy, and Other Poems.*) Most reviews are hostile, offended by

the unpatriotic sentiments or convinced that 'women should not interfere with politics' (*Blackwood's Edinburgh Magazine*). EBB and RB are particularly offended by Chorley's review in *The Athenaeum* of 17 March, including the mistaken view that 'A Curse for a Nation' refers to Britain rather than America.

EBB tells Henrietta that Pen has read all of *PBC* with great approval and was moved to tears by the 'part about Italy' in 'Napoleon III in Italy'.

17   Anna Jameson dies.
20   The Brownings are reading Trollope's *Orley Farm*. They admire its straightforwardness but reprobate its grammar.

EBB is somewhat perturbed about the proposed handover of Savoy to France; French troops have entered Savoy even before voting on the issue has begun.

April
 7   (Sat) EBB writes to SB about the 'blindness, deafness, and stupidity of the English public to Robert'. In England only 'a small knot of pre-Rafaellite men' and John Forster appreciate him. But in America 'he's a power, a writer, a poet. He is read – he lives in the hearts of the people. "Browning readings" here in Boston; "Browning evenings" there. The English prefer lords or "railroad kings" to poets'.
13   EBB sends to Thackeray, who in January had requested a piece for *The Cornhill Magazine* from either RB or EBB, 'A Musical Instrument' (*LP*).

Reports of the royal arrival in Florence prompt her to write 'King Victor Emanuel Entering Florence, April, 1860' (*LP*).

May
18   (Fri) She writes to Fanny Haworth that RB is 'working at a long poem which I have not seen a line of' – probably 'Mr Sludge, "The Medium"' (revised for *DP* in early 1864) – and 'short lyrics which I *have* seen, and may declare worthy of him', presumably some of the shorter pieces in *DP*.

Rome, much riding, and homeopathic medicine have agreed well with RB, on whose 'stoutness' everyone will exclaim on his return to Florence; EBB has never seen such an 'air of *robustness*' in him, she writes to SB in June. At some point during the time in Rome he makes a prose-sketch for what will eventually become *Prince Hohenstiel*.

27   Garibaldi enters Palermo (see EBB's 'Garibaldi'). The Brownings, like most people, have been amazed at his daring assault on Sicily with his 'Thousand'. But to EBB it represents an unwarranted risk: 'the whole good of Central Italy was hazarded by it. If it had not been success it would have been an evil beyond failure.'

June

Probably this month the so-called 'fifth' edition of *AL*, a reprint of the 'fourth', is published.

4   (Mon) – 9 The Brownings travel by vettura from Rome to Florence, spending nights at Viterbo (4), Orvieto (5; here RB admires Luca Signorelli's Last Judgement in the cathedral), Ficulle (6), Chiusi (7), and Siena (8). Soon after their arrival Landor complains about Wilson, who had lost her temper and tried to stop him throwing food out of the window. A rapprochement is with difficulty arranged.

7   EBB's 'First News from Villafranca' (*LP*) appears in *The Independent*, New York, whose editor Theodore Tilton has been impressed by *PBC* and is prepared to pay well (£100 for five short poems).

By mid-month EBB has read George Eliot's *The Mill on the Floss*, which she likes better than *Adam Bede*. She also recommends Anthony Trollope's novels to her brother George (16). RB finds in the San Lorenzo market in Florence the 'Old Yellow Book', containing the principal materials for *The Ring and the Book*, and gives 'a *lira* for it, eightpence English just' (*Ring* I.39).

July

7   (Sat) The Brownings arrive in Siena, again renting Villa Alberti at Marciano. Landor lives nearby with Wilson.

EBB's 'A Musical Instrument' (*LP*) appears in *The Cornhill Magazine*. Her pleasure in the retreat from the heat of Florence is much diminished by worry for Henrietta, who has untreatable cancer of the womb. EBB continues, however, to follow Italian political developments carefully. (Forster, p. 348, suggests that in letters of this period EBB makes 'Henrietta's illness a metaphor for Italy's struggle. She could not think of the suffering of her sister without confusing it with the suffering of "her" country'.)

August
16   (Thurs) EBB's 'King Victor Emanuel Entering Florence, April, 1860' (*LP*) appears in *The Independent*, followed there by 'The Sword of Castruccio Castracani' (*LP*) on 30.

September
W.M. Rossetti and his friend Vernon Lushington visit the Brownings at Marciano. RB meets them at Siena station, shows them Pinturicchio's frescoes in the Libreria Piccolomini, and recommends them to see 'the local museum of paintings'; Rossetti will long remember 'the gusto with which he pronounced the name of "Beccafumi"'. At Marciano the visitors witness one of the frequent near-quarrels over Napoleon III between Landor and EBB and 'some slight symptom of approaching antagonism' in RB 'if Mrs Browning in talking came to the outskirts of the "spiritual" theme'. RB and Lushington discover that they are fellow enthusiasts for the music of the German composer Ferdinand Hiller (1811–85).
27   (Sat) EBB's 'Summing Up in Italy' (*LP*) appears in *The Independent*.

October
Her 'A Forced Recruit at Solferino' (*LP*) is published in *Cornhill Magazine*.
7   (Sun) She draws 'my fig tree' at Villa Alberti, the day before leaving for Florence. 11 and 31 Anthony Trollope, who is visiting his mother and brother in Florence, comes to Casa Guidi. Both EBB and RB

consider him a 'firstrate' novelist; in her opinion *Framley Parsonage* is perfect and its author very English, direct, frank, if ignorantly anti-Napoleonist.

11   EBB's 'Garibaldi' (*LP*) is published in *The Independent.*

26   Garibaldi meets Victor Emanuel.

November

7   (Wed) Garibaldi and Victor Emanuel enter Naples (taken by Garibaldi in September) together.

19–23   The family travels, with EBB in anguished suspense about the fate of Henrietta, via Terni (21) to Rome. They rent at 126 Via Felice (now Via Sistina). During this last visit to Rome RB (if *Ring* I.423 ff. is taken at face value) undertakes some research for *The Ring and the Book.*

December

3   (Mon) News reaches the Brownings of the death of Henrietta at Stoke Court, Thurlbear, Somerset, on 23 November. EBB grieves deeply, and the loss has often been credited, together with the death of Cavour in June 1861, with hastening her own death. She finds some comfort in a letter from Harriet Beecher Stowe (sent on 20 November) dwelling on her faith that her dead son Henry is well and able to communicate with her.

6   EBB's 'De Profundis' (*LP*) is published in *The Independent.*

1861

Her 'A View across the Roman Campagna' (*LP*) is dated '1861'.

January

19   (Sat) RB is 'not inclined to write this winter', EBB tells SB. As in 1858–9, he works much at modelling in clay at Story's studio.

February

Probably this month EBB writes 'Mother and Poet: Turin, After News From Gaeta, 1861' on the loss of the poet

Olimpia Savio's two sons, Alfredo at the siege of Ancona in September 1860, Emilio at the siege of Gaeta in January.

18　(Mon) First meeting of the Italian parliament in Turin.

March

21　(Thurs) EBB's 'Parting Lovers' (*LP*) is published in *The Independent*.

April

2　(Tues) Thackeray writes to EBB to explain delicately that he cannot accept 'Lord Walter's Wife' (*LP*) for *The Cornhill Magazine* since, pure though its moral is, it concerns an 'unlawful passion'; 'our Magazine is written not only for men and women but for boys, girls, infants, sucklings almost' and 'there are things *my* squeamish public will not hear on Monday, though on Sundays they listen to them without scruple'. EBB replies on 21 enclosing instead 'Little Mattie' but arguing that 'the corruption of our society requires not shut doors and windows, but light and air'.

18　She sends to Francesco Dall' Ongaro (1808–73), through Blagden, literal Italian versions of two (unidentified) poems. The idea of his undertaking a verse rendering of her poems on Italian subjects was first proposed in spring 1860.

Probably in April EBB and RB meet (she for the first time) the British consul Joseph Severn, who reminisces about the death of his friend Keats.

May

2　(Thurs) EBB's 'Mother and Poet' (*LP*) is published in *The Independent*, followed on 16 by 'Only a Curl' (*LP*).

21　Shortly before this date (when she sends it to Thackeray for intended inclusion in *The Cornhill*), she writes her last poem, 'The North and the South' (*LP*), after a visit by Hans Christian Andersen. Some time before this Andersen performed 'The Ugly Duckling' and RB 'The Pied Piper' (for which Story played the flute) at a children's party hosted by the Storys at Palazzo Barberini.

c. 25   Alessandri of Rome takes three photographs of EBB and two of RB. (The same photographer took pictures of EBB with Pen, and of RB, in 1860.)

June

EBB's 'Little Mattie' (*LP*) is published in *The Cornhill Magazine.*

  1   (Friday) – 5 The Brownings travel from Rome to Florence via Siena.

  6   Death of Cavour. EBB's shock at the loss of the Italian statesman she most admires and trusts hastens her collapse.

20   EBB's having the windows of Casa Guidi opened is (probably) the cause of the sore throat and racking cough which begin her final decline. During the night of 22–23 RB has her examined by a Dr Wilson, who diagnoses congestion of the right lung and a possible abscess. She, however, maintains that her problem has always been with her left lung and that she feels exactly the same as during the many previous bouts of illness from which she has recovered.

28   Isa Blagden, the Brownings' most regular and intimate visitor at this time, comes in the evening and tells EBB about Baron Ricasoli, the new Prime Minister of Italy, and the beliefs he shares with Cavour.

29   Between 3.00 and 3.30 a.m. RB notices that EBB's feet are cold, and she becomes, briefly, delirious (probably, as a result of an increased dose of morphine). He sends for Dr Wilson, and with the maid Annunziata bathes her feet in warm water and feeds her some jellied chicken. Hearing RB send for more hot water she says 'You *are* determined to make an exaggerated case of it.' Somewhat later he asks if she knows him and she replies 'My Robert – My heavens, my beloved,' kisses him, and says 'Our lives are held by God.' He asks if

she is comfortable and she replies 'beautiful'. A few moments later, at about 4.30 a.m., EBB dies in RB's arms.

Isa Blagden takes Pen to her home, Villa Brichieri, where RB too will spend the nights from 1 July onwards.

July

1   (Mon) EBB is buried in the Protestant Cemetery, Florence. The coffin, with crowns of laurel and white flowers, is carried through the streets. Mourners include Story, Pasquale Villari and Francesco Dall' Ongaro. Shops near Casa Guidi are closed. At the graveside RB reads from EBB's 'The Sleep'.

5   By now, as RB writes to SB, 'Pen, the golden curls and fantastic dress, is gone just as Ba is gone'; he has short hair, long trousers, and 'is a common boy all at once; otherwise I could not have lived without a maid'.

12   Ubaldino Peruzzi, a prominent Florentine and minister in the new Italian government, expresses to RB the hope of 'all the Italians' that, as friends of Italy, he and Pen will not leave Florence; but, RB tells SB, 'we are English, and the beauty of Ba's effort was in its being utterly disinterested and the just zeal of a stranger for right and truth'.

18   EBB's 'The King's Gift' (*LP*) is published in *The Independent*, followed on 25 by 'A View Across the Roman Campagna' (*LP*).

22   RB having tried and failed to have the drawing-room at Casa Guidi photographed, George Mignaty is painting it just as EBB 'disposed it and left it'.

August

1   (Thurs) RB and Pen leave Florence, to which RB will never return, with Isa Blagden. Father and son spend about nine days in Paris at 151 Rue de Grenelle with RB Senior and SB and with them leave, on 12, for St Enogat, near St Malo. Here RB goes for long walks. Pen rides his pony, swims, and sketches.

September

20   (Fri)–21 The group returns to Paris, from which RB and Pen set off for Boulogne on 26.

27   RB and Pen arrive in London to stay with Arabel Barrett at 7 Delaware Terrace.

October

11   (Fri) RB and Pen move into rented accommodation at 1 Chichester Road. Pen begins lessons with a tutor, G.K.Gillespie, designed to prepare him eventually for university entrance.

1862

RB's 'Rabbi Ben Ezra' (*DP*) is probably written in 1862 or 1863.

February

He is elected to the Athenaeum club.

*c.*21   (Fri) RB and Pen go to Paris, spending their time mostly with RB senior, SB, and Milsand. They return to London on 3 March.

March

c. 15   (Sat) RB is offered the editorship of *The Cornhill Magazine* in succession to Thackeray. After some consideration he refuses. Also *c.* 15 he is at dinner with Dickens.

20   (Thurs) EBB's *Last Poems* is published by Chapman and Hall at 6s. Most reviews avoid the more political poems and, like the obituaries of 1861, pronounce her the greatest of women poets.

April

24   (Thurs) RB delivers to Thomas Woolner 'Deaf and Dumb' (*1868*, added to *DP*), on the sculptor's group of the children of Sir Thomas Fairbairn for the 1862 International Exhibition. (RB's verses are for unknown reasons not, in the event, included in the catalogue.)

Some time this month RB meets Ruskin at the National Gallery, where he is working on sketches by J.M.W. Turner.

May

5   (Mon) RB (having, in March, taken out a lease of £92
     10s. per annum), moves with Pen to 19 Warwick
     Crescent, which will be RB's home until June 1887.
     Here, in July, the furniture from Casa Guidi is
     installed. The house is near Delamere Terrace, where
     RB pays daily visits, when they are both in London, to
     Arabel Barrett.

24   With Carlyle he attends the funeral at Broughton
     Castle, Oxfordshire, of Ellen Twisleton. RB has been
     acquainted with her and her husband Edward since
     1852.

June

Early this month RB is given by George Meredith a copy of
his *Modern Love*, a possible influence on 'James Lee' (*DP*).
RB is increasingly moving in society. On 17 (Tues), for
instance, he dines at the house of John and Augusta
Fitzpatrick with guests including Alexander Kinglake. He
receives eight social invitations for 29 alone, but stays at
home then on the first anniversary of EBB's death.

July

18   (Fri) He dines at Lady Marian Alford's. Hatty Hosmer
     is among the guests.

August

2   (Sat) – 3 RB and Pen travel to Paris to join the rest of
     the family and soon afterwards go with them to
     Sainte-Marie, Pornic, Brittany, staying at the house of
     mayor Laraison. Mary Bracken and her son Willy,
     Pen's friend, arrive to stay nearby on 17.

17   RB writes a poem of 120 lines, probably 'Gold Hair: a
     Legend of Pornic' (*DP*). (See also May 1864.) This
     summer he also probably composes 'James Lee' (*DP*)
     and, now or the following summer, 'Dîs Aliter Visum;
     or, Le Byron de nos Jours' (*DP*). At Sainte-Marie he
     wants to 'read, walk, and do nothing but think' – and,
     presumably, to write.

On this or subsequent visits to Sainte-Marie he probably visits the megaliths of Noeveillard, near the road to Pornic (see *Fifine*, lines 2045ff.).

September

19   (Fri) RB makes enquiries through Isa Blagden about another version (the 'Secondary Source') of some of the *Ring* material covered in the 'Old Yellow Book'; by 18 October he has received the manuscript from its owner, a Mrs Georgina Baker who lives near Blagden.

October

2   (Thurs) – 3 The family group returns to Paris, where RB and Pen stay for a week before returning to London (11).

The municipal council of 'grateful Florence' puts up a tablet on Casa Guidi, by the poet Niccolò Tommaseo, remembering EBB as one who in her woman's heart brought together 'the learning of a scholar and the inspiration of a poet' and who made her verse 'a golden ring wedding Italy and England'. (There have been delays in erecting the tablet; RB, already aware of the wording, dedicated EBB's *LP* earlier in the year 'To "Grateful Florence" ... and to Tommaseo ... Most Gratefully'.)

November

10   (Mon) RB visits Dante Gabriel Rossetti at 16 Cheyne Walk and the Carlyles at 5 Cheyne Row, where he talks to Mazzini, incognito in London after the failure of Garibaldi's recent expedition against Rome. He has always liked Mazzini personally, but is impatient with his political 'folly or madness'.

c. 11–15   RB dines with Matthew Arnold.

December

12   (Fri) He dines with Ruskin and meets the painter Edward Burne-Jones and his wife for the first time.

16   RB, following a call from G.H. Lewes, goes to meet George Eliot ('Mrs Lewes') for the first time. 'I liked her much' he tells Blagden.

20 *Selections from the Poetical Works of Robert Browning* (dated 1863) is published by Chapman & Hall, edited by John Forster and Bryan W. Procter. It includes revisions by RB.

1863

January
RB is angered by attempts to gather material from his friends for a biography of EBB. George Stampe of Grimsby, one of the offenders, has obtained the correspondence between her and HSB.

23 (Fri) RB dines with George Eliot and Anthony Trollope.

February
19 (Thurs) He sees somebody every evening, he tells Blagden; today he dines at Lady William Russell's and then goes to Lord and Lady Salisbury's, on 20 to Adelaide Sartoris', on 21 to Lord and Lady Palmerston's.

March
By 3 (Tues) RB has Pen's name entered for residence at Balliol College, Oxford, in 1867. Balliol, where Benjamin Jowett is a Fellow (he will become Master in 1870), impresses RB as a 'reading college'.

10 RB is a member of Charles Dickens' party of fourteen who go to see the 'illuminations' in celebration of the wedding of the Prince of Wales and Princess Alexandra. After four or five miserable, cold hours they succeed in seeing little; besides, 'the English can't manage anything of the kind' compared with the French.

14 RB and Pen go to Paris

At about mid-month EBB's *The Greek Christian Poets and the English Poets* (a reprint of the *Athenaeum* essays of February–August 1842) is published by Chapman & Hall at 5s. It is generally well received but sells much less well than expected.

19 RB, with his sister and son, Milsand, and Willy Bracken, sees *Macbeth* at the Odéon.

29   RB and Pen return to London.

April

Probably towards the end of the month RB, thinking about
Sophie Eckley's falsehood (see August 1859), solaces
himself 'by placing two portraits of her on each side of a
delicious drawing of a "model" in the costume of Truth, just
given to me by Leighton' (letter to the Storys, 2 May).

May

Near the beginning of the month the first volume of RB's
Poetical Works (the 'third' – more correctly second – edition)
is published by Chapman & Hall. The second and third
volumes follow in late June and late August. (RB is paid
£120.) This edition, dedicated to John Forster as the poems'
'promptest and staunchest helper' from first publication,
includes a revised *Sordello* (dedicated to Milsand in honour
of 'one of my deepest affections') and a major redistribu-
tion of poems. Sales are good enough to warrant delaying
the publication of *DP*, intended for later this year, until
May 1864.

21   (Thurs) RB takes Pen to watch the Derby 'privately, by
     going to a friend's house close by the course'.

June

14   (Sun) Richard Monckton Milnes entertains RB, Arnold,
     Froude, G.H. Lewes, Herbert Spencer, Swinburne,
     Ruskin and (as Arnold puts it) 'all the advanced liber-
     als in religion and politics'.

Later in the month RB, Sir George Grove, Dickens, and
Georgina Hogarth are at a 'great dinner-party ... followed
by a musical "at home"' at the house of Frederick and Nina
Lehmann.

July

 1   (Wed) RB, with W.M. Rossetti, visits AT; he dines with
     him on about 10 and they see each other again on 16.
 6   RB tells Milnes, following a conversation on 5, his
     opinion of Swinburne: he doesn't know him well, likes
     him much, and feels that poems he recently heard him

recite are 'moral mistakes, redeemed by much intellectual ability'. It is 'a shame' that Chapman has given RB's
comments as a reason for rejecting Swinburne's work.

19   EBB's former maid, Annunziata, visits RB and Pen. She
remains in England and serves successfully in various
'great houses'. Later in the day RB talks to Anthony
Trollope at the Cosmopolitan Club, Charles Street, of
which he has recently become a member. (In later
years RB goes there very rarely; he will resign in 1883.)

27   RB calls on Eliot and Lewes. He is reading the first two
volumes of Eliot's *Romola* (1863), which he tells her in a
letter of 2 August is 'the noblest and most heroic prose-
poem that I have ever read'. But the third volume will
disappoint him: the 'delinquencies' of Melema are too
much dwelt on while 'Savonarola and the Republic,
which I expected would absorb attention and pay for
the previous minutenesses, dwindled strangely' (to
Blagden, 19 October).

August

2   (Sun) RB and Pen leave London for Paris, where they
stay for a week. With SB and RB Senior they go on to
Tours on 9 and Nantes and Sainte-Marie on 10. As in
1862 they rent the mayor's house. Mary and Willy
Bracken arrive on 20, by which time he has read and
been deeply disappointed by Flaubert's *Salammbô*
(1862), lent him earlier by Mary Bracken.

September

In the first part of the month RB reads Paul Féval's *Annette
Laïs*, serialised in *L'Opinion nationale*, and finds it 'delicious
… delicate and witty'.

October

3   (Sat) RB Senior and SB return to Paris with RB and
Pen, who proceed to London on about 10.

November

19   (Thurs) RB has recently read Ernest Renan's *La Vie de
Jésus*, one of the books of 'Higher Criticism' (with

Strauss's *New Life of Jesus* of January 1864) which he may be answering in 'A Death in the Desert' (*DP*). Much of the poem may, however, have been written some time before this. Renan figures in the 'Epilogue' to *DP* which is composed some time between now and early 1864.

December
RB sees Thackeray twice in the early weeks of the month. He fails to appear at a dinner on 23 (Wed); at another dinner to which Thackeray has also been invited, RB learns that he has died. His 'defects were quite noticeable enough, but of a kind to let the goodness *show through*: and I am rather struck to find how much I must have liked him, these many years'.
Late in the year RB works on reducing Story's two-volume *Roba di Roma* (Chapman & Hall, 1863) for an edition in one volume.

1864

February
12 (Fri) RB makes his will, mostly in favour of his sister and son. AT and Palgrave are witnesses.

March
 8 (Tues) Date given by RB to his 'Very Original Poem, written with even a greater endeavour than ordinary after intelligibility, and hitherto only published on the first leaf of the author's son's account-book'.

April
 3 (Sun) RB's 'Orpheus and Eurydice' ('Eurydice to Orpheus; a Picture by Leighton' in *Selections*, 1865; *1868*), is published in the catalogue of the Royal Academy Exhibition.
 4 George Eliot 'called on Fred Chapman [the publisher] and saw Browning there'.
At the end of the month RB's 'Gold Hair: a Legend of Pornic' (*DP*) appears in *The Atlantic Monthly* for May 1864.

22   He meets Garibaldi at the American consulate in London and, later, dines with Dickens, Wilkie Collins, and Forster at Greenwich.

May

He calls on AT.

14   (Sat) Julia Wedgwood sends her first letter to RB. (They first met in the spring of 1863 and again this April.)

c. 25   Publication in *The Atlantic Monthly* for June 1864 of 'Prospice' (*DP*; written at some point since EBB's death) and 'Under the Cliff', section VI of 'James Lee' (*DP*, in *1868* as 'James Lee's Wife').

28   Publication of RB's *Dramatis Personae* by Chapman & Hall at 7s. The American edition is published by Ticknor & Field. Reviews are at last prevailingly favourable (*The Athenaeum* on 4 June calls him 'a great dramatic poet' and emphasises the originality of one whose 'music is not as the music of other men'). Sales are good. Later in the year a second impression includes three stanzas (lines 101–15) added to 'Gold Hair' in response to George Eliot's desire for a clearer explanation of the presence of the gold coins in the coffin.

June

30   (Thurs) William Allingham lunches at Warwick Crescent. Topics of conversation include Tennyson, 'Mr Sludge' and Daniel Home, and 'Sullivan, Gounod, etc'. RB says that he wishes often that he could go to an opera or play instead of a party, that he would rather write music than poetry and that he 'longs also to be a sculptor; "If one could only live six hundred years, or have two lives even"'. In the afternoon RB calls on Julia Wedgwood. They have recently been corresponding about her state of mind and religious perplexities following the last illness and death of her brother.

July

7   (Thurs) RB presents Wedgwood with a copy of EBB's *LP*. On 13 he gives her *Greek Christian Poets* and the new edition of her *Poems*.

28   He meets the Swedish soprano Jenny Lind at Lady Westmorland's house in Wimbledon.

In late July or possibly early August he dines with Edward John Trelawny, whom he first met in 1844. In a busy social season RB has attended many social functions but 'the infinitely best thing in London to me is the *music*'. He knows Charles Hallé and Joseph Joachim and makes them play when he meets them at parties. Recently he heard Hallé play Beethoven's 'wonderful last Sonata – the 32d – in which the very gates of Heaven seem opening'.

August

3   (Wed) RB and Pen join RB Senior and SB in Paris for a week. The party then travels to south-western France, to Arcachon, St Jean-de-Luz, and Biarritz, all of which they find crowded, before settling at Cambo-les-Bains, near Bayonne. In the south RB is saddened by reminders of Italy.

20   At the Pas de Roland, a mountain pass, RB lays out 'the full plan of his twelve cantos' for *The Ring and the Book*. (This is what he tells W.M. Rossetti in March 1868; his recollection of placing a pebble for each book on a parapet in Florence in 1860 is much later. Clearly planning develops sporadically over a period of four years in 1860–4.)

September

13   (Tues) The group moves on from Cambo, via still-too-crowded St Jean de Luz, to Maison Gastonbide, Biarritz. The town is 'crammed with gay people, of whom I see nothing but the outsides', and there are superb sea, sands, and views.

17   Death of Walter Savage Landor. RB, refusing to accept paintings willed to him by Landor, tells Isa Blagden in October that 'I have been more than rewarded for my poor pains by being of use for five years to the grand old ruin of a genius, such as I don't expect to see again'.

19   RB writes to Blagden that he is attending to his new poem, 'the Roman murder story', and that 'the whole

is pretty well in my head'. He is also reading much Euripides.

26 He spends a day in Spain, visiting Fuenterrabia, Irun, and San Sebastián

October

7 (Fri) – 9 The party travels from Biarritz to Paris via Bayonne, Bordeaux, and Tours. On 11 RB and Pen reach London, where RB begins sustained work on *Ring*.

Soon after his arrival he reads AT's *Enoch Arden* volume, sent while he was abroad. (He already knows 'Enoch Arden' itself. On 2 September he told Wedgwood, in some detail, how he would have written it.)

14 RB dines with Milnes (now Lord Houghton) and others.

17 He writes to Leighton, who is in Rome, for information on the church of San Lorenzo in Lucina (to be used in *Ring* Book Two).

November

10 (Thurs) RB calls on Eliot and Lewes and tells them about the discovery, in Florence, of a terracotta bust of Savonarola.

1865

January

28 (Sat) Ruskin expresses the view, in a letter to RB, that 'Mr Sludge' is an abuse of his talents; if mediums are fraudulent then this should be stated in plain prose. RB replies on 30 'I don't expose jugglery, but anatomize the mood of the juggler.'

February

c. 15 (Wed) RB sees AT.

By mid-month RB has sent his selection from his own work, to be published in the *Moxon's Miniature Poets* series in 1866, to James Bertrand Payne of Moxon's.

March

Publication of RB's *Poetical Works*, 4th edition, in three volumes.

1   (Wed) Julia Wedgwood writes to say that her friendship with RB has been wrongly interpreted and that it will be best if they do not meet, at least not at her house. He decides to stop seeing her altogether, admitting only in a letter of 17 March 1867 that he 'underwent great pain from the sudden interruption of our intercourse' and does not understand why it was necessary. For her, she says on 26 March 1869, near the end of their correspondence, their friendship was and is 'the great blessing of my life'.

17   He meets the traveller and writer Emily Eden (1797–1869) at Lady Cowper's.

21   He appends this date to the preface of *A Selection from the Works of Robert Browning*, to be published in September.

April

18   (Tues) – 28 RB and Pen are in Paris. RB is present at Milsand's wedding and also introduces him to Matthew Arnold, who is inspecting Continental schools.

June

10   (Sat) – 12 RB goes to Oxford to meet Benjamin Jowett and discuss Pen's Balliol prospects. The poet strikes Jowett as open, sensible, and knowledgeable.

July

29   (Sat) RB and Pen go to Paris.

August

From early August the Browning group again stays in the mayor's house at Sainte-Marie, and the Brackens again take a house nearby. Little has changed (the village 'is its dirty, unimproved self') except that the old church of Pornic is being demolished and some Norman features of the church in Sainte-Marie are being removed. During this visit (or perhaps in 1862 or 1863) RB visits the Fair of St Gilles in Pornic and conceives or sketches *Fifine*.

September
In Sainte-Marie RB rereads George Eliot's *The Mill on the Floss* (he has also been reading and enjoying Trollope's *The Belton Estate* as it comes out in *The Fortnightly Review*), supervises Pen's reading of *The Aeneid*, and corrects his Greek translations.

At the end of the month *A Selection from the Works of Robert Browning* is published by Moxon.

October
1   (Sun) The group leaves Brittany. They travel via Angers, Le Mans, and Chartres to Paris; RB is back in London on about 7.
15   Eliot and Lewes visit 19 Warwick Crescent. RB shows them EBB's 'chair, tables, books etc ... her Hebrew Bible with notes in her handwriting, and several of her copies of the Greek dramatists with her annotations'. Eliot says she has seen nothing so interesting since Goethe's house.

November
1   (Wed) RB has completed about 15 000 lines of *The Ring and the Book*. (Progress will slow in 1866.)

December
4   (Mon) He dines with Forster, Alexander Dyce, and Jane and Thomas Carlyle on the occasion of the latter's seventieth birthday.
5   *A Selection from the Poetry of Elizabeth Barrett Browning* is published by Chapman & Hall (dated 1866). The first collected edition of EBB's *Poetical Works* is the so-called 'seventh' (1866).
12   RB sees AT. They meet several more times this month.
By mid-month the monument to EBB designed by Frederick Leighton has at last, after many delays and alterations, been erected in the Protestant Cemetery in Florence.

1866

January

Towards the end of the month *The Poetical Works of Robert Browning*, 3 vols, is published by Chapman & Hall.

February

10 (Sat) RB has dinner with the Tennysons. On 17 he is with AT and Carlyle at Lady Stanley's reception.

15 He dines with Lord Dufferin.

22 Date given by RB to his manuscript Latin poem 'On Being Defied to Express in a Hexameter: "You Ought to Sit on the Safety-Valve"'.

March

14 (Wed) He dines with Trollope, Frederick Chapman, and the proprietors and staff of *The Fortnightly Review*.

31 He goes to Paris, where his father is ill.

April

14 (Sat) He returns to London.

18 Jane Carlyle dies.

28 RB visits the exhibition of the Royal Society of Painters in Water Colours to see works by Alfred Hunt including 'Childe Roland to the Dark Tower Came'.

May

G.F. Watts' portraits of RB and of AT are shown in the Royal Academy Exhibition.

19 (Sat) RB agrees with Blagden that Italians are uninteresting 'as thinking, originating souls ... I always said they *are* poetry, don't and can't write poetry ... but as a nation, politically, they are most interesting to me'. His 'liking for Italy was always a selfish one, – I felt alone with my soul there' whereas in England hundreds of his acquaintance 'walk up and down in the lands of thought I live in'.

June

2 (Sat) – 4 RB and Pen again visit Jowett at Balliol.

12–13   RB rushes to Paris on hearing from his sister that their father is dying; he dies on the morning of 14. 'So passed away this good, unworldly, kind hearted, religious man, whose powers natural and acquired would have so easily made him a notable man, had he known what vanity or ambition or the love of money or social influence meant ... He was worthy of being Ba's father'. On 16 he is buried in Père Lachaise cemetery. SB comes soon afterwards to live with her brother in London.

19   RB returns to London. On 20 he informs Frederick Chapman that he intends to change publishers. (His dealings with Chapman & Hall, especially obtaining accounts from them, have long been complicated. Sales have remained poor. RB's decision is also influenced, in some degree, by Isa Blagden's dissatisfaction with the company as publishers of her novels). Smith, Elder will from 1868 publish the works of RB and EBB. Over the next few years RB becomes intimate with George Smith, the managing director, who pays and publicises him well and who organises many business and personal matters for him. On Fridays RB often attends the supper-parties given by George and Elizabeth Smith at Oakhall Park, Hampstead.

July

27   (Fri) RB, SB and Pen sail to Jersey where they visit Frederick Tennyson. (The original intention was to go to Guernsey and, with the aid of an introduction from Houghton, meet Victor Hugo.)

August

c. 1   (Wed) The Brownings proceed to Brittany. Having found Dinard unsuitable and spent a few days at St Malo (from which they visit Mont-St-Michel and Dinan) they are established by 7 at Le Croisic in the large Maison du Bochet. (The Brackens as usual take a house close by, and Anne Egerton Smith stays at 'the Bathing Establishment' from late August.) From the house can be seen Guérande, where members of the party dine at an inn, 'Les Guérandaises'. RB remembers reading (originally in or before 1839) a description of the area in Balzac's *Béatrix*. He tells George Barrett that Le Croisic is wild, solitary, and has good bathing. It is also 'the old head-seat of Druidism in France' where 'the people were still Pagan a couple of hundred years ago … and the women used to dance around a [still upright] phallic stone' (cp. 'The Two Poets of Croisic' (*Saisiaz*), lines 105ff.)

October
Early in the month RB, SB, and Pen travel to Paris. They reach London three days later.
18   (Fri) G.H. Lewes calls on RB.

November
Milsand stays with RB (until 29). Together they dine at Arnold's on 8 (Thurs) with Houghton and others, are visited by Ruskin on 13, and dine with him on 19.
19 and 20   RB is at 'a horrid place called Clerkenwell, there to make part of a Grand Jury'.

1867

January
15   (Tues) RB calls on Ruskin.
At the end of the month Jowett asks whether RB is interested in standing as the next Professor of Poetry at Oxford, but he lacks the necessary Oxford MA and the authorities are not at present prepared to confer one on him. He would have accepted the chair, he tells Blagden, for Pen's sake – in the hope of 'standing well' with the university. His first lecture would have been on Thomas Lovell Beddoes.

February
c. 15   (Fri) He encounters Macready, now old, changed, 'uninterested in his old life' and living in retirement with his second wife.

March

Some time during this 'season of dinners' RB dines with Lord John Russell and William Ewart Gladstone, who talk 'unreservedly'.

25 (Mon) Pen goes to Oxford to stay with Jowett for a week. Jowett having found him able enough in Latin but not in Greek, RB arranges for the attempt to gain a place at Balliol to be delayed.

April

21 (Sun) William Allingham lunches with RB and SB. RB tells him that Swinburne's verses are 'a fuzz of words'.

May

After much renewed work in April–May, RB has completed 18 000 lines of *Ring*.

6 (Mon) RB dines at the Garrick with a group including Forster, Lewes, Trollope, Sir James Fitzjames Stephen, and George Meredith.

12 He dines with Jenny Lind and her husband Otto Goldschmidt.

14 Professor John Stuart Blackie (1809–95) calls on RB and finds him 'an active, soldier-like, direct, rather stout little man – a fine contrast to the meditative ponderosity of Tennyson'.

22 RB, writing to Isa Blagden, wonders how he would feel if he saw familiar places in Italy again: the past feels generally 'as if it had been pain. I would not live it over again, not one day of it. Yet that seems my real *life*, – and before and after, nothing at all: I look back on all my life, when I look *there*: and life is painful.'

June

14 (Fri) – 17 He visits Oxford. On 18–19 Jowett comes to London to tell him that the University of Oxford is to confer on him the degree of MA by diploma, apparently an exceptional honour. He feels that this, and the Honorary Fellowship at Balliol which Jowett tells him

will follow, will be an advantage for Pen (and an excuse for seeing or checking up on him) when he goes to Oxford; he is also aware that his poetry is more popular in Oxford than elsewhere. The degree-giving ceremony takes place on 26.

July

c. 5 (Fri) RB takes 'the three loveliest women in London' to hear Anton Rubinstein play, but makes an excuse to leave them afterwards since, unlike friends from the past, 'Ladies This, That and the Other are of this present time which wearies me' (to Blagden, 19 July).

He calls on Edward John Trelawny in Brompton.

c. 27 RB, SB, and Pen go to Paris, where they see the Exposition Universelle.

August

1 (Thurs) The Brownings stay again at Maison du Bochet, Le Croisic, near the Brackens and, from about 12, Annie Egerton Smith. Some time in August or September the whole party visits the wild coastal village of Piriac, where an encounter with an old man reflecting on the relics of an abortive tin- and silver-mining enterprise of fourteen years ago reminds RB that 'the imaginative men are not exclusively the poets and painters, as Balzac knew well enough'.

RB takes great pleasure in swimming. (In youth he could swim only a few strokes; he has made much progress on his recent French holidays.)

September

30 (Mon) He writes or completes 'Hervé Riel' (*Pacchiarotto*), the source of which, Caillo jeune's *Notes sur le Croisic* (1842), he and SB read probably this summer, perhaps last. Also at this time, probably, RB reads Gustave Grandpré's *Promenade au Croisic* III (1828), source of 'The Two Poets of Croisic' (*Saisiaz*).

Pen is rumoured to have fathered two illegitimate children by local girls during this holiday.

October

At the beginning of the month RB, SB, and Pen travel via Paris to London, arriving *c.* 5 (Sat).

RB becomes an Honorary Fellow of Balliol College, Oxford.

Pen goes to Oxford to study with his tutor, Reginald Broughton. Later he attends Jowett's lectures and studies with Robinson Ellis of Trinity College. He is also much involved in rowing.

16 Swinburne's article on Arnold for *The Fortnightly Review* prompts RB's satirical lines on Swinburne as little man and great lyre/liar.

23 RB dines with Frederick and Nina Lehmann.

November

19 (Tues) RB is with Arnold at the Athenaeum. They often see each other; RB is particularly pleased that at his request Arnold has reprinted *Empedocles on Etna*, for the first time since 1852, in his *New Poems* (published in July).

December

For some weeks an unfounded rumour that RB is to marry the poet Jean Ingelow has been circulating.

1868

January

19 (Sun) Baron Christian von Tauchnitz calls on RB to try to persuade him to reconsider his decision not to allow publication of EBB's and his own work in the popular Tauchnitz series. RB has no desire 'to give cheap shillings' worths to the travelling English'. (He will change his mind in December 1871, allowing Tauchnitz to publish two volumes of each poet's work in 1872.)

RB longs to be in Italy, 'out of all this ugliness', refuses as many dinner invitations as possible, and gets up at 5 a.m. to work on *Ring*.

February

20–21 (Thurs–Fri) He visits Balliol for the first time as an Honorary Fellow.

March

29 (Sun) He dines with Lord and Lady Russell.

This spring RB's *Poetical Works* is published in six volumes by Smith, Elder. It includes *Pauline* (reprinted for the first time since 1833 and purely, according to the preface, in order to forestall a pirated edition), the revised *Strafford*, and the reorganised *MW* and *DR*. Smith pays RB £600.

April

2 (Thurs) Pen fails his matriculation examination at Balliol.

May

23 (Sat) – 25 RB visits Balliol.

26 He shows Allingham the 'Old Yellow Book'. He says he offered the story to various friends. He 'offered it to Anthony Trollope to turn into a novel, but T. couldn't manage it'.

June

10 (Wed) RB hears Anton Rubinstein play at a private party.

11 Arabel Moulton-Barrett dies (of heart disease) in RB's arms at 7 Delamere Terrace, London.

July

30 (Thurs) RB is still uncertain what to call *Ring*; he prefers 'The Franceschini' to 'The Book and the Ring'. With SB he sets off for Paris, where they stay at 156 Rue St Dominique with Mme Louis, who helped nurse RB Senior in his final illness.

August

c. 5 (Wed) RB and SB go to Brittany: to Vannes, Auray (whence there are excursions to Carnac, Locmariaquer, and Ste Anne d'Auray), Brest, Morlaix, St Pol de Léon, Roscoff (which they find too full), Quimper, and at last (*c.* 11) settle an inn at 'niched Audierne, a delightful quite unspoiled little fishing town, with the open ocean in front' and woods and hills behind. Annie Egerton Smith also comes to stay in Audierne.

26 RB and SB go by pony-cart to see, on a hill by the sea, the procession and festivities for the Pardon of Saint Anne. (A smaller 'Pardon' takes place in Audierne on 2 September.)

28 They go on a four-hour walk to Pont-Croix and the church of Notre Dame de Confort.

September
At about the beginning of the month Pen goes to St Andrews with Jowett's reading party, returning on 8 October. It becomes clear to Jowett that Pen is unlikely material for Balliol.

October
c. 5 (Sat) RB and SB leave Audierne. After a second brief stay in Paris with Mme Louis, they are back in London by 9.

November
5 (Tues) RB sends Julia Wedgwood the first two volumes of *Ring* two weeks before publication. She is the first to see them apart from George Smith and his wife. (Milsand has read the first volume.) He briefly floats the idea that Wedgwood should visit SB so that they can meet again. On 15 she writes to him about the *Ring* volumes, arguing that he has allowed undue predominance to his interest in evil; on 19 he admits that it is a fault of his nature to 'unduly like the study of morbid cases of the soul' but maintains that in this poem he is attempting to explain '*fact*'.

19 AT reads RB *The Holy Grail*. RB tells him that it is his 'best and highest' work.

20 RB reads to AT from Book One of *Ring*; AT finds it 'full of strange vigour and remarkable in many ways; doubtful whether it can ever be popular'.

21 *The Ring and the Book*, volume one, is published by Smith, Elder, at 7s. 6d. RB has received £1250 from Smith for five years' right to publish the work.

December

1 (Tues) The first of the two volumes of the American edition of *The Ring and the Book* is published (from revises sent by RB on 30 October) by Fields, Osgood; the second volume follows on 1 March. James T. Fields pays RB £200. The poem does not sell well in America.

c. 10–14 Sophie Eckley visits RB. She denies a rumour that she has been showing people her letters from EBB. She offers to give them to him immediately, and has willed them to him or Pen. 'Hence, on the whole, I conclude that this particular devil is not quite so black as she has been painted, by myself, amongst others' (to Blagden, 17).

22 RB writes a letter of condolence to Forster on the death of his sister. This, and Forster's reply of 25, ends a second period of estrangement between them. (For the first see 22 June 1844; see also 1870 and December 1875.)

26 *The Ring and the Book*, volume two, is published by Smith, Elder, at 7s. 6d.

27 RB shows Allingham the 'Old Yellow Book' a second time and also the proofs of 'Pompilia' and two rings of soft gold. He praises his own poem.

1869

January

15 (Fri) Pen, having continued to study in Oxford during the autumn, matriculates at Christ Church, a considerably less academic college than Balliol.

19 RB lunches with Prince and Princess Christian at the Deanery, Westminster, with Dean Arthur Stanley and his wife Lady Augusta Stanley.

29 He attends the first of a series of poetry readings by Robert Buchanan at the Queen's Concert Rooms, Hanover Square.

30   *The Ring and the Book*, volume three, is published by Smith, Elder, at 7s. 6d. Wedgwood (who received her copy on 21) continues perturbed by the poet's 'readiness to hold a brief for any character or feeling, so it is only individual'.

February

12   Wedgwood receives her advance copy of the fourth volume of *Ring*. She likes the Pope's speech, in which there is more of what 'seems to me your special message to us … than in anything else you have written', but she still regrets that 'so large a part of your canvas is spent in delineating what is merely hateful'. The correspondence continues, with some rather awkward discussion of the rift between her and RB in 1865, until the spring, and is briefly renewed in June and July 1870.

14   (Sun) George Eliot and G.H. Lewes host a gathering of friends, including Palgrave, Mark Pattison, and Frederic Harrison, where RB 'talked and quite admirably à propos of versification'.

27   *The Ring and the Book*, volume four, is published by Smith, Elder, at 7s. 6d.

March

13   (Sat) RB, Carlyle, the geologist Sir Charles Lyell and the historian George Grote are presented to Queen Victoria by Lady Augusta Stanley at tea in the Deanery, Westminster.

April

RB is offered and refuses the Lord Rectorship of St Andrews University.

He has met, and likes, the novelist (and, subsequently, Egyptologist) Amelia B. Edwards.

14   (Wed) RB and SB travel to Paris, where they stay at the Hôtel du Nord. During their month's visit they see much of Milsand and visit Fanny Haworth twice at Versailles.

On 15 RB sees Sophie Eckley, by 19 he has met Gustave Doré (who 'seems a very pleasant clever fellow, but not at all the man to do a great thing'), and subsequently he meets Ernest Renan and the painter Jean-Léon Gérôme.

May

13 (Thurs) RB and SB return to London. On 15 they go to Oxford to see Pen cox the Christ Church boat.

June

c. 10 (Thurs) – 12 Swinburne calls on RB. He finds his poetry florid, containing 'the *minimum* of thought and idea in the *maximum* of words and phraseology' (to Blagden, 22 March 1870) but remains on friendly terms with him.

July

10 (Sat) RB dines with Louisa, Lady Ashburton (whom RB and EBB first met, as Louisa Mackenzie, in 1851).

31 RB, SB, Pen, and the Storys depart for Scotland.

August

RB and SB are in Edinburgh for three days and then go to Abbotsford with the Storys. RB feels exhausted and unwell until they arrive at Lady Ashburton's estate at Loch Luichart on about 20 (Fri). Here, at some point, the subject of marriage between RB and Ashburton is mentioned. Almost certainly it is she, not as used to be generally believed he, who proposes or at least raises the matter. Full details are not, however, known. Relations between the two remain apparently cordial until 1871.

September

5 (Sun) RB sends his Round Robin ('Dear Hosmer; or still dearer Hatty …') in a letter to Hatty Hosmer. (The poem is signed by RB, Lady Ashburton, and her other guests, but is evidently wholly or mostly his.)

10 By this date RB has moved on from Loch Luichart. He goes with the Storys (while SB and Pen return to England) to visit George and Rosalind Howard, later the Earl and Countess of Carlisle, at Naworth Castle in

Cumberland, where Story draws him reading from 'Pompilia'. At Naworth Edith (Edie) Story tells Rosalind Howard that in Scotland Lady Ashburton made it abundantly clear that she was in love with RB and also claims that RB is in fact in love with her, Edith Story. He is back in London by about 26.

October

In mid-October he tells Blagden, mysteriously, that he has travelled eight hundred miles in three days 'on an emergency'.

He is furnishing the rooms next to Jowett's in Balliol which have been his since June. (Not having used the rooms for a single night, however, he relinquishes them to help the crowded college in May 1870.)

In the last week of this month RB visits Lord and Lady Stratford de Redcliffe at their house near Chertsey.

November

13   (Sat) RB goes to Blickling Hall, Norfolk, to stay with the Marquess of Lothian.

c. 19   He moves on to Earl and Countess Cowper at West Park, Ampthill, Bedfordshire, and then to the Earl of Carnarvon at Highclere Castle in Berkshire, returning to London by 23.

25   Pen fails his preliminary examinations.

December

25   (Sat) RB and Carlyle are entertained by the Forsters.

1870

In the early 1870s (probably before the end of 1872) RB and Forster quarrel once more. At the house of Ernest and Lily Benzon (10 Kensington Palace Gardens) Forster angers RB by casting doubt on a story, told him by a woman friend, about negligence in the household of the Princess of Wales; RB suddenly seizes a decanter and, according to Rudolf Lehmann, says 'Dare to say one word in disparagement of

that lady and I will pitch this bottle of claret at your head!'
They remain unreconciled until December 1875.

January
RB's disillusion with Shelley, as a person at least (see June
1856), is furthered when he reads W.M. Rossetti's biographical introduction to his edition of 1870.

19 (Wed) RB, discussing *The Holy Grail and Other Poems*
(1869) in a letter to Blagden, contrasts his psycholo-
gical interests with AT's more picturesque emphasis:
AT 'thinks he should describe the castle, and effect of
the moon on its towers, and anything *but* the soul'.
Like William Morris ('sweet, pictorial, clever always')
he has become monotonous. Anne Thackeray's much
praised *To Esther and Other Sketches* (1869) is poor
stuff.

February
At about the beginning of the month Pen surprises his
father by breaking out 'in violent poetry' in the shape of 'a
poem in some six hundred lines about an adventure he had
at Croisic'.
Milsand stays with the Brownings between mid-February
and mid-March.

April
SB goes to Paris, returning by about 13 May.
At about mid-month RB dines at Sir Frederick Pollock's
with Anthony and Rose Trollope and the Benzons.

26 (Tues) RB writes the sonnet 'Helen's Tower' for the
Marquess of Dufferin, who is building a tower at
Clandeboye in memory of his mother Helen, Lady
Dufferin and Countess of Gifford, who died in 1867.
AT too gives Dufferin a 'Helen's Tower'.

May
19 (Thurs) RB tells Isa Blagden (in a letter dated '19 June')
that D.G. Rossetti's poems are 'poetical ... *scented* with
poetry'. His 'school' is effeminate.

June
Pen, having failed the re-takes of his first examinations, leaves Christ Church. During the last five weeks he has spent at least £150.

July
c. 2	(Sat) – 4 RB visits Jowett at Balliol College, Oxford.
13	He travels to Scotland for the funeral of the Marquess of Lothian. He returns on 14–15.
19	France declares war on Prussia. RB hopes that Italy will gain Rome as a result and feels that 'in the interest of humanity' Napoleon III 'wants a sound beating this time and probably may get it'. The Emperor will be the subject of *Hohenstiel*, written mostly in August–October 1871.
RB often mentions at this time the possibility of going back to Italy, usually with the proviso that Florence would be too painful. Rome and Naples are several times suggested.

August
Pen having developed measles in July, RB and SB delay their departure for France until 10 (Wed).
12	They take a house 'of the most primitive kind' by the sea at St Aubin-sur-Mer, Calvados, Normandy. From Milsand, who owns a cottage here, RB hears a few details of the suicide of Antoine Mellerio on 13 April. (See August 1872.)
'The sadness of the war' – which the French are losing – 'and its consequences go far to paralyse all our pleasure.' But 'the French have been wrong as well as foolish', he tells Blagden on 19. All able-bodied men have left St Aubin. Milsand, while remaining as kind as usual, is despondent. But in spite of everything RB manages much swimming and visits Caen, Bayeux, and various unspecified châteaux.

September
1	(Thurs) The French are defeated by the Prussians at Sedan. On 2 Napoleon III becomes a prisoner-of-war. Milsand persuades RB and SB to leave (*c.* 25) as Prussia

invades and the situation becomes more dangerous. Having been unable to leave from Le Havre they manage to join a cattle-boat at Honfleur.

October
2 (Sun) The Romans agree, by plebiscite, to the annexation of their city by the Kingdom of Italy. (It was captured on 20 September.) Pope Pius IX, refusing to acknowledge the new state, becomes 'the Prisoner of the Vatican' and the subject, doubtless soon afterwards, of RB's 'The Dogma Triumphant'.

1871

January
2 (Mon) Pen goes to stay with Lady Ashburton at Melchet Court. RB courteously declines to join his son.
Robert Buchanan's poem *Napoleon Fallen* is published and, probably soon afterwards, read by RB.
26 Armistice ends the Prussian siege of Paris. At about this time RB writes 'Mettle and Metal' for Lady Charlemont.

February
28 (Tues) 'Hervé Riel' (*Pacchiarotto*) is published in *The Cornhill Magazine*. RB departs from his usual dislike of periodical publication in order to raise money (George Smith of Smith, Elder gives him 100 guineas) for the relief fund for the starving people of Paris.

April
23 (Sun) RB, Trollope, Burne-Jones, and Ivan Turgenev lunch with Eliot and Lewes.
c. 30 SB, troubled by a persistent cough, goes to stay with friends in Homburg until the end of May.

May
c. 18 (Thurs) RB dines with Lord Lytton (formerly Sir Edward Bulwer-Lytton). On 20 he spends the day with Lord John Russell at Richmond, and on 23 is at dinner with Lytton and the French ambassador, the Duc de Broglie. RB is much

in demand, refuses many invitations, but goes out more than he would otherwise, he claims, because 'it stings such vermin as little Austin [his enemy the poet Alfred Austin] to the quick that I "haunt gilded salons"' (to Blagden, 21 May).
27   He departs on an unidentified brief country visit.

June
Early in the month Milsand comes to stay, leaving on about 15 July.

July
RB refuses a request from the students of Glasgow University that he should stand for the Lord Rectorship. He finally refuses a third entreaty (coming mainly from the 'young liberals') late in September.

August
 8   (Wed) RB's *Balaustion's Adventure* is published by Smith, Elder at 5s. It sells out in about five months and is reprinted in 1872 and 1881.
 8   RB and Pen set off for Scotland. (SB goes to France, staying with the Milsands at St Aubin or Dijon and, in September-October, in Paris). They stay in a shooting lodge on the estate of RB's friend Ernest Benzon at Milton House, Glen Fincastle, Perthshire. Until late afternoon when they go to the house, Pen is mostly out shooting game while his father is alone at the lodge with piano and books. From mid-month he works regularly on *Hohenstiel*. They see Jowett and Swinburne, who are staying nearby with a reading-party.

September
30   (Sat) RB concludes *Hohenstiel* with line 1908. The remaining lines are added by 7 October (according to RB's note on the MS at Balliol College) and delivered to Smith, Elder, after minor corrections, on 8 November.

October
 2   (Mon) Reluctantly, RB visits Lady Ashburton at Loch Luichart. Other guests include Lord and Lady

Houghton. (RB is among those who are accommodated that night at Brahan Castle.) It may well be on
this occasion that, Ashburton having raised the question of marriage once more, RB speaks of his heart
being buried in Florence and the only attractiveness of
such a marriage being the (social and financial) advantage to Pen (RB to Edith Story, 4 April 1872). As a result
she 'foamed out into the couple of letters she bespat-
tered me with' in 'all the madness of her wounded
vanity' (to W.W. Story, 19 June 1886).

12   RB arrives back in London.

December

16   (Sat) RB's *Prince Hohenstiel-Schwangau, Saviour of Society*
is published by Smith, Elder at 5s. It sells 1400 copies in
the first five days but sales then gradually peter out.
RB believes that Napoleon III 'in the main … meant to
do what I say' [in the poem]; 'I thought badly of him
at the beginning of his career … better afterward, on
the strength of promises he made. … I think him very
weak in the last miserable year'.

RB begins writing *Fifine at the Fair*. On 29 he reports to
Blagden that he is half-way through the poem (in spite of
the fact that he is 'beset with letter-writers, two thirds of
whom are unknown to me').

27   Having read the first volume of Forster's Life with its
revelations about Dickens' childhood, he includes in a
letter to Emily Pattison his satirical lines 'In Dickens,
sure, philosophy was lacking …'

1872

January

c. 11   (Thurs) He is visited by Kate Field, the American
writer who first met him and EBB in 1859.

RB is unwell and Pen more seriously so with an attack of
rheumatism which confines him to his room until about
15 February.

23 RB is at dinner with Sir Henry Taylor (1800–86), administrator and author of the verse play *Philip van Artevelde* (1834), to whom James Spedding introduced him last December.

25 He has 'just all but finished' *Fifine*; but see 30 March.

29 He breakfasts with the Attorney General, John Duke Coleridge, and goes to court with him to hear part of his address to the jury in the case of Arthur Orton, the 'Tichborne Claimant'.

In January or February RB first meets Eliza FitzGerald ('Mrs Thomas FitzGerald'), who will become a good friend and regular correspondent for the rest of his life. When she is in London, at 22 Portland Place, he often visits her on Sunday afternoons before going on to Mrs Procter and Carlyle.

February

16 (Fri) Death of Henry Chorley. 'I probably ought to have made more allowances for his individuality,' RB writes to H.G. Hewlett on 16 April 1873.

18 RB dines with the banker Julian Goldsmid and his wife Virginia.

19 RB arranges to pay Elizabeth Wilson, who is in financial difficulties, £10 every 1 March.

c. 25 Milsand arrives in London on a visit which lasts until early April. 'No words can express the love I have for him' RB tells Isa Blagden on 30; 'he is increasingly precious to me'.

March

4 (Mon) Alfred Domett, who has just returned from New Zealand after thirty years, lunches with RB, SB and Milsand. The friendship is renewed, although it is less close than before Domett emigrated.

30 RB has, over the last two months, experienced *Fifine* '*growing* under me'. It is finished in early April.

30 He departs on a week's country visit to Lord Brownlow at Belton House in Lincolnshire.

April

4   (Thurs) RB, in a letter to Edith Story, contrasts the continued friendliness to him of Brownlow's mother Lady
Marian Alford in spite of her intimacy with Lady
Ashburton – she understands that 'there are two ways
of telling a story' – with Hatty Hosmer's readiness to
believe slanderous stories about him and to take up
Ashburton's defence while failing to ask him for his
version of events. As a result RB 'has done with Hatty,
for once and always'. (He will be angered by her
attempt at reconciliation in a letter of 4 April 1887.)
Other guests include Lady Cowper, the dedicatee of
Balaustion.

April

5   (Fri) Lady Ashburton joins the party at Belton; on 6 RB
leaves. According to Mary Gladstone everyone supposed he was proposing to her: 'at least she let it be
thought so'. Subsequently RB sees 'every now and
then that contemptible Lady Ashburton, and mind[s]
her no more than any other black beetle – so long as it
don't crawl up my sleeve' (to the Storys, 9 June 1874).

6   RB, Eliot, and Lewes are among the guests for dinner
and music at Lady Castletown's.

May

11 (Sat) RB finishes work on the proofs of *Fifine*.

14 He dedicates *Selections from the Poetical Works of Robert
Browning* to AT as 'In Poetry – Illustrious and
Consummate; in Friendship – Noble and Sincere'.

c. 18   RB arrives at Alton Towers, Cheadle, as the guest of
the nineteenth Earl of Shrewsbury. He returns to London
on 27.

c. 20   Blagden, in ill health, comes to England (until
September).

June

4   (Tues) *Fifine at the Fair* is published by Smith, Elder at
5s. Dante Gabriel Rossetti, to whom a copy is sent on

4 or 5, is convinced that he and his *Jenny* (1870) and 'The Blessed Damozel' are being satirised. He sees RB as part of a conspiracy against him, of which the most obvious manifestations are the attacks of Robert Buchanan, author of 'The Fleshly School of Poetry – Mr D.G. Rossetti' (in *The Contemporary Review* for October 1871). RB agrees, at least privately, with Buchanan's opinions. Rossetti breaks off relations.

Most reviewers receive *Fifine* with some bafflement.

At the end of the month RB dines at the Marquess of Ripon's and the following day with Jowett 'and so the horse goes round the mill!'

July

4   (Thurs) He goes to Harrow for Speech Day.

26   He sets off on a brief unidentified country visit.

August

6   (Tues) He again visits the Earl of Shrewsbury at Alton Towers for a few days.

c. 14   RB and SB travel as in 1871 to St Aubin. (Pen has gone to Scotland). From Milsand they learn more of the case of Antoine Mellerio, whose will, contested by his relatives, was upheld in court at Caen on 9 July. Through Milsand he obtains legal documents, questions local people, visits the scene of Mellerio's death at Tailleville, and, pondering this 'capital brand-new subject for my next poem', conceives *Red Cotton Night-Cap Country.* Anne Thackeray is staying near St Aubin at Lion-sur-Mer, where RB comes to seek reconciliation with her after she has allegedly spread rumours about his possible second marriage. According to the poem, which is dedicated to her in 1873, she calls the area by the 'fast/Subsiding-into-slumber sort of name' (lines 143–4) 'White Cotton Night-Cap Country'. (The poem plays much on the contrast between this impression and the bloody 'red' tale as well as the French Revolutionary associations of the red cap.)

22   Coronation of the Virgin ceremony at La Délivrande: see *Red Cotton,* ll. 443 ff. RB does not attend, but visits

the church soon afterwards and probably reads about the occasion in *Le Journal de Caen et de la Normandie* (Gridley, pp. 272–3).

September

14 (Sat) RB, SB, and the Milsands leave St Aubin for Paris, where they see Alexandra Orr. Milsand is 'wanted for his vintage' at home near Dijon, and RB and SB decide not to distract him by accompanying him. Instead they take lodgings at 11 Rue St Louis, Fontainebleau, on 19. Here they walk in the forest and RB reads Greek drama, especially Aeschylus.

October

2 (Wed) Annie Egerton Smith comes from Paris to visit RB and SB.

20 RB and SB return to London.

November

2 (Sat) RB thanks AT for *Gareth and Lynette* (to be published in December), and asks him to read Alfred Domett's New Zealand epic *Ranolf and Amohia* (1872).

December

1 (Sun) RB begins writing *Red Cotton Night-Cap Country.* This month the *Official Guide* of the Chicago and Alton Rail Road begins serialisation of RB's works in the belief that the travelling public 'will prefer works of permanent value, which appeal to the highest culture and most refined taste'. The series will end, incomplete, in June 1874.

1873

January

20 (Mon) Isa Blagden dies in Florence. In June RB is much annoyed to hear that a volume of her poems is to be edited by his enemy Alfred Austin, who first attacked RB (given his 'trumpery tinsel wreath' by 'large London salons') in *The Temple Bar* for June 1869 and then in *The Poetry of the Period* (1870). RB caricatured

Austin as 'Dogface Eruxis, the small satirist' in *Aristophanes' Apology*, line 1674.

23 RB finishes *Red Cotton Night-Cap Country.*

March

8 (Sat) He sends his publisher George Smith an 'Advertisement' (not used) for *Red Cotton* stressing, as a defence against possible charges of libel, that he has used only the 'published pleadings' and decisions of a court of law. Smith and RB remain concerned and seek advice on 15 and 26 from two lawyers, the second of whom is the Attorney General, John Duke Coleridge. In the meantime, in the set of proofs dated 15 March, RB replaces the real names of places and people with fictional ones.

31 He receives corrected proofs of *Red Cotton* and reads 'as much as may prove digestible at a sitting' to its dedicatee Anne Thackeray.

April

Milsand stays with RB and SB.

May

RB's *Red Cotton Night-Cap Country or Turf and Towers* is published near the beginning of the month by Smith, Elder at 9s.

9 (Fri) Anne Thackeray by now is embarrassed by press objections to the sordid subject-matter of *Red Cotton*. RB is keen for Smith to publish in one of his magazines – the *Cornhill* or *Pall Mall* – Alexandra Orr's account of the poem and its morality, which he has not read but knows will be more favourable. Smith does not take Orr's article, which appears instead, later in the month, in *The Contemporary Review* for June.

June

4 (Wed) RB writes to James T. Knowles, editor of *The Contemporary Review*, praising the unprecedented fairness, intelligence, and conscientiousness of Orr's review.

c. 11   He dines with the Trollopes.

July
31   (Thurs) RB and SB leave for France.

August
 2   (Sat) They again take the house at St Aubin. RB walks around Tailleville (the Clairvaux of *Red Cotton*) but finds 'nothing material to alter in the poem'.
12   RB and SB visit the châteaux of Fontaine-Henri and Creully and the priory of St Gabriel.

RB is reading Aristophanes and much else of or on Greek drama.

September
14   (Sun) RB's friend Ernest Benzon dies at Allean House. RB and SB hear the news a few days later on their arrival in Paris from St Aubin. They return to London on about 30. Benzon bequeathes to RB a valuable collection of mostly oriental weapons.

October
RB sees the Tennysons several times. AT introduces him to F.J. Furnivall at about this time (certainly by early December). He will soon become a frequent visitor to 19 Warwick Crescent.

November
c.15   (Sat) – 22 RB is among the guests of the Earl of Carnarvon at Highclere Castle.

R.H. Horne's 'Letters from Elizabeth Browning to the author of "Orion" on Literary and General Topics' begins to appear, with RB's permission, in *The Contemporary Review* (for December 1873 and January, February, and April 1874).

December
12   (Fri) RB declines (but see 5 March 1879) the Presidency of the New Shakspere Society offered by Furnivall, who has already approached AT without success.
19   RB dines with the Tennysons.

1874

January

Pen has (encouraged by John Everett Millais) decided seriously to take up painting. He studies, at the suggestion of Felix Moscheles, in Antwerp under Jean-Arnould Heyermans.

25   (Sun) RB calls on George Eliot.

February

 3   (Tues) Domett records in his diary how RB, dining with the Misses Swanwick of Regents Park, affirms his optimism in 'a lively discussion as to good or evil preponderating in human life generally' with Frances Power Cobbe (1822–1904), writer and campaigner for women's rights and other liberal causes.

10   Furnivall and John Seeley, Professor of Modern History at Cambridge, lunch with RB and SB.

16   RB is considering writing a poem on Gladstone's problems with his opponents within the Liberal party. Furnivall encourages him in this idea: 'Victorian life is the thing' and will interest future readers.

March

10   (Tues) RB, Eliot, Lewes, and George and Rosalind Howard, dine with the Colviles; guests including Joachim and the cellist Alfredo Piatti then perform.

June

 8   (Mon) RB is at a dinner with the American ambassador General Robert Schenk and a party where he talks to James Russell Lowell.

17   He completes the 'Transcript' from Euripides' *Herakles* which will be incorporated in *Aristophanes' Apology*.

August

 4   (Tues) RB and SB leave London. From *c.* 11 they stay, with Annie Egerton Smith, at Mers-les-Bains, Picardy, in Maison Robert. This, Alexandra Orr will note, is the last house 'of the straggling village', standing 'on

a rising cliff. In front was the open sea; beyond it a long stretch of down; everywhere comparative solitude'.

11 About now RB begins work on the main body of *Aristophanes' Apology*, finishing it on 7 November.

October

5 (Mon) Bryan Waller Procter dies.

November

10 (Tues) RB and SB leave Mers. They go to Antwerp to visit Pen before returning to London *c*. 16.

December

28 (Mon) Replying to a letter of 27 from Frances Power Cobbe, RB assures her of his support for anti-vivisectionism (later expressed in verse in 'Tray', *Idyls* (I).

1875

Probably this year William Grove becomes RB's manservant (until 1882, when he becomes a photographer). According to Grove's later account the regular pattern of RB's day is to rise at 7.00, read until 8.00, breakfast at 9.00, work 10.00–1.00, lunch briefly before going out to call on friends or go to art shows, and come home to dress for dinner by 6.00. On Tuesday and Friday afternoons he visits Alexandra Orr and on Saturdays goes to the Athenaeum.

Some time this year RB dines with Mary (Mrs Humphry) Ward.

March

4 (Thurs) RB, George Eliot, and G.H. Lewes are at Frederick and Nina Lehmann's for a musical evening where the performers include Joachim and Piatti.

April

15 (Thurs) *Aristophanes' Apology* is published by Smith, Elder at 10s. 6d. Domett, like a number of critics,

remarks on 'the large demands Browning makes in this book on his reader's knowledge', but RB will not countenance adding notes. He concludes the matter by saying 'it could not be helped, but he was not likely to try anything of the sort again'.

May
8   (Sat) RB probably attends the opening night of a production of Wagner's *Lohengrin* (in Italian) at Covent Garden.

June
1   (Tues) RB starts writing *The Inn Album*, completed on 1 August.
3   RB and the Italian actor Tommaso Salvini dine with Eliza FitzGerald.
30 AT has recently sent RB a copy of his *Queen Mary*. (See 18 April 1876.)

July
RB sees and approves of Salvini in *Hamlet*.
8   (Thurs) RB goes to Lady Airlie's garden party. Among the many other guests are the Queen of Holland, Lewes, Herbert Spencer, and Jenny Lind.
16 RB dines with Lord Stratford de Redcliffe.
23 RB sees AT.

August
14 (Sat) RB and SB leave London to visit Pen at Dinant in Belgium, where he is continuing to study under Heyermans.
c. 21–22   SB goes to Paris to stay with the Milsands. RB goes to Villers-sur-Mer, staying at Villa St Ange with Annie Egerton Smith. He works on the proofs of *The Inn Album* and swims regularly. On 25, with Egerton Smith, he goes to Beuzeval.

October
RB visits the Château de Bonneville.
25 (Mon) He leaves Villers for London.

November

14 (Sun), 21, 28 *The Inn Album* is published in three parts in *The New York Times*, and on 19 by Smith, Elder in book form (7s).

29 RB writes or completes 'Bifurcation' (*Pacchiarotto*).

December

1   (Wed) John Forster writes to say how *The Inn Album* has moved him and to re-state his old affection. RB replies on 2, praising Forster as his best of critics and claiming that he has never doubted his good will, and their third and final breach is healed.

28 He writes or completes 'Pisgah-Sights. I' (*Pacchiarotto*).

1876

January

12 (Wed) While out walking RB speaks with Gladstone, Trollope, Lord Coleridge and the historian Lord Acton.

15 RB writes or completes 'At the "Mermaid"' (*Pacchiarotto*).

18 He tells Edmund Gosse, who has dedicated his *King Erik* to him, that he admires its 'dramatic power and … understanding management of character'.

February

Psyche Apocalypté: a Lyrical Drama Projected by Elizabeth Barrett Browning and R.H. Horne is published in *The St James's Magazine and United Empire Review.*

1   (Tues) RB writes or completes 'House'; 'A Forgiveness' follows by 5, 'Shop' by 11, 'Pisgah-Sights. II' by 19, and 'Fears and Scruples' by 26 (all in *Pacchiarotto*).

3   Death of John Forster. RB is relieved that he was reconciled with his old friend and champion two months ago.

March

1   (Wed) Death of Lady Augusta Stanley. RB, John Lothrop Motley, and the Earl of Shaftesbury are

among the pall-bearers at her funeral in Westminster Abbey.

4 RB writes or finishes 'Magical Nature' and perhaps 'Natural Magic' (*Pacchiarotto*); 'Saint Martin's Summer' follows by 27.

10 On encountering Allingham at Hyde Park Corner, he tells him of Disraeli's hypocrisy – saying one thing in his speech and the opposite afterwards to him – at the Royal Academy dinner. (See also 4 January 1878 and 18 February 1881.)

24 RB is at Mrs Benzon's for dinner and music with Lewes, Joachim, Leighton, and the Lehmanns.

April

6 (Thurs) RB writes or completes 'Appearances' (*Pacchiarotto*). He visits Allingham, tells him about his recurring dream of nearly reaching Asolo, and reads approvingly from Allingham's copy of Quarles' *Emblems*. They also talk about music; according to RB no musically untrained listener can appreciate Beethoven, where 'instead of a melody in a song or ballad, you have, in the harmonies and transitions, countless melodies melted and flowing and mingling'.

15 Between now and 1 May RB writes 'Of Pacchiarotto, and How He Worked in Distemper' (*Pacchiarotto*).

18 RB goes to the first night of AT's *Queen Mary* at the Lyceum. He particularly admires Henry Irving's Philip.

24 RB writes or finishes 'Epilogue', on 25 'Numpholeptos' and on 28 'Cenciaja' (*Pacchiarotto*).

May

19 (Fri) RB writes, with the other pieces for *Pacchiarotto* already in press, 'Filippo Baldinucci on the Privilege of Burial'.

20 Tommaso Salvini calls on RB.

23 RB, Lewes, Charles Hallé, Salvini, and Julia Cartwright dine at Mrs Benzon's.

June

10 (Sat) Alfred Austin's unconvincing 'Disclaimer', in *The Examiner*, disowns most of his attacks on RB.

July

c. 1 (Sat) RB goes to Balliol and then to stay with Eliza FitzGerald at Shalstone, Buckinghamshire, until 10.

13 He sees Trollope, who tells him of his dislike for Eliot's *Daniel Deronda*.

18 RB's *Pacchiarotto and How He Worked in Distemper: With Other Poems* is published by Smith, Elder at 7s. 6d. It includes attacks on RB's critics and especially Austin.

August

3 (Thurs) RB and SB set off from London for Blairbeg House, Lamlash, Isle of Arran. Annie Egerton Smith is with them again. RB walks each day for two hours before breakfast, reads, and walks or drives after dinner.

28 RB, attempting to console FitzGerald for the mental illness of her son Robert, says that he has always believed – with Schopenhauer, he has recently become aware as a result of reading Helen Zimmern's 1876 Life – that 'the soul is above and *behind* the intellect which is merely its servant'.

October

23 (Wed) RB and SB return to London.

December

8 (Fri) Following massacres by the Turks in Bulgaria (the subject of Gladstone's *The Bulgarian Horrors and the Question of the East* of 6 September) RB is among the many notable conveners – others are Darwin, Trollope, Froude, Ruskin and G.O. Trevelyan – of the National Conference on the Eastern Question at St James' Hall.

21 RB thanks AT for a copy of his *Harold*, singling out for praise 'the scene where Harold is overborne to take the oath'.

1877

January

16 (Tues) – 18 RB visits Oxford. On 17 he attends the celebration dinner for the opening of a new building at Balliol. Among the many illustrious diners are the Archbishop of Canterbury, the Bishop of London, the Dean of Westminster (RB's friend Arthur Stanley), Lord Coleridge, Matthew Arnold, and the Marquess of Lansdowne.

February

Early this month RB and George Smith investigate the possibility of publishing a translation of Aeschylus' *Agamemnon* with pictures of Schliemann's excavations and finds at Mycenae. This proves impossible but by 10 (Sat) he is fairly sure that he will, in any case, go ahead with the translation. He starts work probably between now and early March.

28 RB and AT are photographed for a new periodical, *The Portrait*.

March

8 (Thurs) RB attends the Cambridge degree ceremony at which Joseph Joachim is made Doctor of Music, and the concert given by him on 9. He is at Trinity College for much of 9 as the guest of Sidney Colvin, Slade Professor of Fine Art; here RB, Joachim and others 'had a warm controversy on the subject of Beethoven's last quartets. The member of the party who talked most and knew least about the subject was, curiously enough, Browning' according to Charles Villiers Stanford. He goes home on 10.

April

23 (Mon) RB finishes his *Agamemnon*.

May

RB writes the preface to his *Agamemnon* (published with date 1 October), indicating that Carlyle encouraged the project. In the event, however, Carlyle finds the translation obscure; 'He picks you out the English for the Greek word by word ...'

21 (Mon) RB composes, in unknown circumstances, the impromptu 'Wagner gave six concerts ...'

June

4 (Mon) Probably with Annie Egerton Smith, his usual companion at concerts, he attends Anton Rubinstein's last recital of the season at the Crystal Palace.

July

28 (Sat) RB and Story meet at the Athenaeum.

August

7 (Tues) RB and SB leave for Paris. From 9 they stay, with Annie Egerton Smith and Gustave Daourlans, at La Saisiaz, a chalet near Collonges in Haute-Savoie. RB visits Rousseau's Bossey ('Bossex') and (on 31) Voltaire's Ferney. His reading includes Homer and a work or works by Franz Grillparzer (given him by Eliza FitzGerald; he has been reviving his 'acquaintance with German'). RB and Egerton Smith are much involved in discussion of a series of articles in *The Nineteenth Century* for June–September on 'The Soul and Future Life'. The discussions and the articles will, after her death, contribute to 'La Saisiaz'.

September

Pen has been considering marrying a Belgian woman, probably (the evidence for the whole affair is very scanty) daughter of the owner of a hotel in Dinant, the Tête d'Or. RB is highly displeased, mainly on the grounds that Pen lacks a substantial income of his own and will be distracted from his profession. The relationship is broken off and reconciliation between father and son brought about by Milsand.

14 (Fri) RB and SB find Annie Egerton Smith dead in her dressing-room shortly before their mountain walk was due to begin. While waiting for her sister to arrive from Paris he organises the 'formalities to be observed

here' which 'are precise and troublesome'. Egerton Smith, who is buried at Collonges on 16, was 'one of the most devoted friends I ever had in my life ... I have been much favoured in friendships – especially from women: no one was ever more disinterestedly devoted to me who grieve to remember how little I was ever able to do in return for so much'.

19   RB climbs Mont Salève, which he was going to do with Egerton Smith on the day of her death.

20   RB and SB leave for Paris. 'I could not tell the incidents of that memorable week more faithfully in prose and as an accurate account of what happened [than in 'La Saisiaz'] ... I could proceed to nothing else till I had in some way put it all on paper' (letter to Rev. John D. Williams, 30 January 1880). They return to London by the end of the month.

October
15   (Tues) RB's *The Agamemnon of Aeschylus* is published by Smith, Elder at 5s.

November
 9   (Fri) RB completes 'La Saisiaz' (*Saisiaz*) in 'London's mid-November' (line 606).

10   Between now and 8 December he writes 'The Two Poets of Croisic'.

17   Professor William A. Knight writes to ask RB to accept nomination for the Lord Rectorship of St Andrews University. A deputation of students is warmly received in Warwick Crescent on 20, but RB sends his apologetic refusal on 22.

December
 4   (Tues) RB admits to Carlyle – Carlyle claims to Allingham on 5 – that 'all said' his *Agamemnon* 'was of no use'.

15   RB spends £3. 10s. on a ring for 'A' (very probably Alexandra Orr).

26   RB, Eliot and Lewes, and Leighton and his sister Alexandra Orr dine at Mrs Benzon's.

1878

January

15 (Tues) RB writes the epilogue to 'The Two Poets of Croisic'.

February

12 (Tues) Lord Houghton gives a lunch-party for RB, Eliot, Lewes, Kinglake, Sir Charles Dilke, and the American poet Louise Chandler Moulton.

28 With Gladstone and the Duke of Argyle RB is a witness at the wedding of Lionel Tennyson.

March

26 (Tues) RB invites AT, Carlyle, W.M. Rossetti, Houghton, and others, to come to Warwick Crescent before 31 in order to see Pen's painting *A Worker in Brass.*

30 RB goes to a gathering at the Tennysons'. Gladstone, Arnold, and Allingham are also there. Joachim plays.

April

 3 (Wed) RB, Disraeli, and Princess Louise are among those dining with Percy Wyndham. On 4 Disraeli writes to Lady Bradford of RB as 'a noisy, conceited poet' and says that 'all the talk [was] about pictures and art, and Raffaelle, and what Sterne calls "the Correggiosity of Correggio"'.

 4 RB, AT, and Edward Burne-Jones are among the guests at a breakfast given by Gladstone. During a discussion on Disraeli's 'Jingoist' Eastern policy, RB delivers impromptu lines against Disraeli – 'We don't want to fight …'

19 Eliot and Lewes dine with RB.

May

15 (Wed) *La Saisiaz: the Two Poets of Croisic* is published by Smith, Elder at 7s. Reviews are generally more enthusiastic than they have been for any work by RB since *Balaustion's Adventure.*

June
5 (Wed) RB goes to a large social gathering at Lord Carnarvon's.

He attends the banquet given to the President and Council of the Royal Academy by the Dulwich Picture Gallery.

July
8 (Mon) Some time after this date RB sees Henry Irving in Leopold Lewis' *The Bells*.

He is learning Spanish. By 9 August, he tells FitzGerald, he can 'read ordinary prose well enough, and Calderon with no great difficulty'.

27–30 He visits Offington, Worthing, the home of Thomas Gaisford.

August
6 (Tues) – 7 RB organises the photographing of Pen's *A Worker in Brass* (which was shown in the Royal Academy exhibition) and its despatch to Joshua Fielden of Stansfield Hall, Todmorden, who has paid £300 for it.

13 RB and SB leave for Paris. They then travel, by way of Bad Ragaz and the Engadine, to Splügen in Switzerland where they stay at Hotel Bodenhaus. They enjoy four- or five-hour walks to Hinterrhein and the top of the Splügen pass. Nowhere has agreed with RB better, he writes to Mrs Charles Skirrow, and he is now convinced that 'mountain air, – and not the sea-bathing, – is my proper resource when fagged at the end of a season'. Here RB writes the two *Dramatic Idyls* poems 'Ivàn Ivànovitch' and 'Ned Bratts'. The remaining poems in the volume are probably written here, in Italy, or in London this Autumn.

September
3 (Tues) RB and SB go on a longer excursion to Hinterrhein, returning to Splügen on 6.

23 RB and SB leave Splügen and journey to Lecco via Chiavenna, Colico and Bellagio. SB is in Italy for the first time and RB has not been here since 1861.

24 They go on to Verona and *c.* 26 to Treviso and Asolo,
which he first knew more than forty years ago and has
always longed to see again. (See also 6 April 1876.) In
'this very primitive place' they stay at 'the most unso-
phisticated of inns', the Stella d'Oro. Short of reading
matter, he can find only a volume of short stories, *Alla
fenestra*, by Enrico Castelnuovo whom he later meets
in Venice. On 28 they visit Possagno and look at
Canova's water-colours which are 'a wonder of
detestability'.

October
4 (Fri) They go on to Venice (Albergo dell' Universo).
17 They leave, via Padua, Milan and Brescia, for Paris and
are in London by 22.

November
6 (Wed) RB buys a 1771 edition of Bunyan's *Works*. He
drew on *The Life and Death of Mr Badman* from memory
when writing 'Ned Bratts' in August.

December
18 (Wed) RB writes, or the classical scholar J.P. Mahaffy
receives from him, 'Oh Love, Love ...', a translation of
lines from Euripides' *Hippolytus* (in Mahaffy's *Euripides*
(1879)).

1879

RB provides 'The blind man to the maiden said ...' for
anonymous inclusion in Clara Bell's translation of
Wilhemine von Hillern's *The Hour Will Come, the Tale of an
Alpine Cloister* (1879).

January
18 (Sat) RB is present, as a sponsor, at the christening of
Alfred Browning Stanley Tennyson, son of Lionel
Tennyson and grandson of the poet, in Westminster
Abbey. RB's friend Dean Stanley officiates; if he were
not otherwise engaged this evening he would, as

usual, dine with Stanley and 'afterward help him do the honours of the Abbey to the tradesmen who assemble for tea in large numbers'.

March

12 (Wed) RB accepts Furnivall's renewed offer of the Presidency of the New Shakspere Society.

26 Paintings by Pen Browning are on show at 17 Queen's Gate Gardens, South Kensington, an empty house lent by RB's publisher George Smith. As usual RB promotes his son's work and invites friends to come and admire it. On this occasion they include AT (with whom RB dines several times this spring), Carlyle, and Domett.

April

28 (Mon) *Dramatic Idyls* is published by Smith, Elder at 5s. It sells well enough for the issue of a second edition in 1882.

June

9 (Mon) – 11 RB is in Cambridge to receive the honorary degree of LLD from the university.

12 He is present, as a defence witness (questioned on 14) when R.H. Shepherd, who has published *The Earlier Poems of Elizabeth Barrett Browning* – those which are out of copyright – brings a suit against *The Athenaeum* for calling him such names as 'insect' and 'literary vampire'. RB states his agreement with *The Athenaeum* and objection to the edition, but Shepherd is awarded damages.

14–16 RB visits Jowett at Balliol College, Oxford. Dinner guests include the novelist Rhoda Broughton (1840–1920). Later, at RB's suggestion, some of the party walk in the moonlit quadrangle and RB talks intensely to a seventeen-year-old, Eveline Farwell, mainly about Goethe's 'theory … that it was Judas Iscariot's intense faith in Christ which led to his betrayal of Him …'. She has found his anecdotes at dinner trivial, but now feels that she sees 'the real man'.

25 He visits Houghton.

August
13 (Wed) RB and SB leave London. They stay in the mountains again, at Cortina d'Ampezzo.

September
They stay again at Albergo dell' Universo, Venice. Either this year or the following the Storys introduce RB, on the Lido, to Daniel Sargent Curtis (1825–1908) and his wife Ariana (1833–1922), Americans resident in Venice of whom he will see much on subsequent visits.

October
RB and SB arrive back in London in late October or early November.

December
20 (Sat) They dine with the artist Gustav Natorp (b. 1836), whom RB will see and correspond with frequently in the 1880s.

1880

January
9 (Fri) RB dines (as he did last January) with the barrister and musician Arthur Duke Coleridge and his wife Mary.
20 'Piero of Abano' (*Idyls (II)*) is dated thus in the Balliol manuscript at line 416. The remainder is added at some point during the next few months.
28 RB writes, to accompany a picture by Pen, 'The Delivery to the Secular Arm: a Scene During the Existence of the Spanish Inquistion at Antwerp, 1570'.

February
2 (Mon) 'Echetlos' is completed, as by 22 is 'Muléykeh' and by 27 'Clive' (all in *Idyls (II)*).
3 RB sees AT's *The Falcon* at St James' Theatre.

March

From early this month Thomas and Emma Hardy begin visiting Anne Procter at Albert Hall Mansions, where they often meet RB on Sunday afternoons.

10   (Wed) RB finishes 'Doctor – ' (*Idyls (II)*).

21   In a letter to John H. Ingram he refuses, 'for reasons of insuperable force to me', to give 'any assistance whatever to the writer of the biography [of EBB] which your publisher projects'. If RB's friend Helen Zimmern (1846–1934) had written such a work, he 'would have so far strained a point in favour of a person for whom I have the very highest esteem as to correct any material error in her manuscript'. He does not oppose the writing of such a volume, he tells Ingram on 5 May 1882. Ingram's biography will be published by W.H. Allen in 1888.

26–29   Four paintings by Pen are on display at 11 Queen's Gate Gardens.

29   (Easter Monday) RB dines with the Tennysons and Dean Stanley.

April

 9   (Fri) 'Pan and Luna' (*Idyls (II)*) is completed. The prologue and epilogue are probably written in April or May.

20   The manuscript of *Idyls (II)* is sent to press.

May

 7   (Fri) RB dines with Natorp.

June

 3   (Thurs) He attends a performance of Aeschylus' *Agamemnon* in the new hall at Balliol (AT is also there), walks to college gardens and libraries with Jowett, and returns home on 4.

6–22   SB is in Paris, at first with Pen.

c. 10 RB dines with Lord Carnarvon.

12   RB shows paintings by Pen at 11 Queen's Gate Gardens to Lord Coleridge and his family and to James Russell

Lowell, goes to Arthur Duke Coleridge's musical party, dines at Sir Matthew and Lady Ridley's, and ends the evening at a party given by the Duchess of Cleveland; '"thus runs the world away". Yet people are kind, and I cannot bear to seem ungracious and ungrateful'.

15 *Dramatic Idyls, Second Series* is published by Smith, Elder at 5s.

17 RB has recently read John H. Ingram's *Edgar Allan Poe: his Life, Letters, and Opinions* (1880), sent by the author.

July

13 (Wed) RB is reading the fourth volume of Alphonse Karr's *Le Livre de bord* (1879).

26 RB is at tea with Lady Knightley and a group of friends. He reads them some of his poems.

August

10 (Tues) RB and SB go to Paris. On 13 they continue to Lyon and Grenoble, from which on 14 they visit the Grande Chartreuse. SB, as a woman, cannot enter the monastery proper, and RB finds it on the whole disappointing; there is 'anything but a *conventual* behaviour on the part of the multifarious guests, who make merry as at an eating-house, in a mean-looking room' and the tour is crowded and hurried. But the monks' life remains evidently simple and there is a good library. RB's father could happily have embraced this sort of life; so, 'in *one* mood possible to my mind', could he (letter to FitzGerald, 4 September). And now, having sampled it, he will no longer refuse 'a *petit-verre* of Chartreuse after coffee!'

16 RB and SB arrive at 'a minute country inn grandiloquently styled' Hôtel Colomb at Lans, a 'rural quiet unspoiled' hamlet south-east of Grenoble. Here they enjoy walking and a general sense of well-being.

September

19 (Sun) Writing to FitzGerald, RB says that he must soon open the box containing his love-letters to EBB, reread

them 'for the first and last time', and destroy both them and her letters to him. 'However other people feel differently, and the destruction of such crowns and palm-branches will be hard to bear, no question – hence the postponement of it.'

20   RB and SB leave Lans for Grenoble and proceed on 21 to Turin, where they see the national art exhibition, thence to Genoa (*c.* 23), Milan (*c.* 25), and Venice, where from 28 they again stay at Albergo dell' Universo. They spend time with the Storys and a number of other Americans, the Layards, Alexandra Orr (who leaves Venice by 13 October), and RB's publisher George Smith and his wife and daughters.

October

11   (Mon) RB and SB go by gondola to Torcello, Burano, San Francesco 'and other islets'. On the same day Sir Austen Henry Layard shows them round his house, Palazzo Capello, where they will dine on 14.

12   They dine with an American family whose cook is Ferdinando Romagnoli, who produces for them 'a genuinely Tuscan dinner' and is delighted to see RB again.

13   RB is at Ca' Alvisi, the home of Katharine de Kay Bronson, a wealthy American expatriate to whom he has recently been introduced, probably by Story. In the evening RB and SB go to a production of Paisiello's *Il barbiere di Siviglia* (1782), revived at the Teatro Rossini 'as a musical curiosity'. Richard Wagner is also in the audience. (Wagner 'was a great genius but greater curmudgeon ... a monster of peacock-like vanity', he will tell Bronson after Wagner's death in 1883.)

14   RB writes 'Thus I wrote in London, musing on my betters ...', as an explanatory addition to the epilogue of *Idyls (II)* ('Touch him ne'er so lightly ...'), in the album of Edith Bronson.

28 RB and SB leave Venice for Ferrara, Bologna, Ravenna, Turin, and Paris.

November

7   (Sun) They reach London.
9   RB is at the Lord Mayor's banquet at the Mansion House.
17 RB calls on Carlyle. He is now silent unless spoken to, 'but when he does speak all the old soul is in the little he says'. John Tyndall, superintendent of the Royal Institution, also visits.
19 RB dines with James Russell Lowell and meets his second wife Fanny.
24 He reads or rereads *AT's Ballads, and Other Poems* (1880) at breakfast.
27 He has just finished G.O. Trevelyan's *Early History of Charles James Fox* 'and cannot go with his glorification of that scapegrace's early days'.

December

22 (Wed) George Eliot dies. RB attends her funeral on 29.
30 He attends the wedding of Lord Wentworth and Mary Stuart Wortley.

1881

January

1   (Sat) RB inspects newly arrived pictures by Pen, calls on Millais, goes to the Old Masters show at the Royal Academy, and dines with Lady Stanley of Alderley.
26 J.O. Halliwell-Phillipps, ally of Swinburne against Furnivall and his New Shakspere Society, writes to RB to protest about attacks on him by Furnivall. RB politely disclaims involvement in the doings of the society; the presidency is purely honorary. But Halliwell-Phillips writes again (31) and calls on RB in order to press his point.
c. 29 RB dines with AT.

In January or early February RB reads George Sand's
Correspondance, volume one (1881).

February
RB, tired of the 'tangle of facts and fancies' people continue to publish about his life, agrees to let Edmund Gosse
'take down some notes of my life'. For about a month
Gosse comes to Warwick Crescent once a week. (The
resulting article will appear in *The Century Magazine* for
December.) As on several other occasions RB reveals to
Gosse a side of himself rarely glimpsed by others at this
time: 'To a single listener, with whom he was on familiar
terms, the Browning of his own study was to the
Browning of a dinner party as a tiger is to a domestic cat.'
His voice ranges from a shout to a whisper as he walks
around his study or drawing-room, 'a redundant turmoil
of thoughts, fancies, and reminiscences flowing from those
generous lips'.

4   (Fri) or 5? RB goes to AT's *The Cup* at the Lyceum.
5   Carlyle dies.
c. 5–7   The five new pictures by Pen are shown at 11
Queen's Gate Gardens.
13   RB is at Eliza FitzGerald's London home, 22 Portland
     Place.
14   Halliwell-Phillipps angers RB by publishing the letters
     between them on the New Shakspere Society as
     Correspondence with Robert Browning (first seen by RB
     on 4).
18   RB dines, at Lord Airlie's, with Arnold and Disraeli.
     The day after Disraeli's death on 19 April RB will
     claim to FitzGerald that on this occasion he 'sat by
     him at dinner and admired his vivacity and good
     nature ... I always liked his works and had an interest
     in himself'. He will attack Disraeli once more in the
     'Parleying With George Bubb Dodington' (*Parleyings*,
     1887).

Late this month Swinburne breaks with RB over his refusal
explicitly to condemn, as President of the New Shakspere

Society, Furnivall's personal attacks on Swinburne and on Halliwell-Phillipps.

March

27 (Mon) Domett, Layard, and Oscar Wilde ('foppishly dressed', observes Domett) are among those viewing Pen's Royal Academy pictures. This summer Wilde will send RB his *Poems* (1881).

April

23 (Sat) RB has recently received proofs of Sidney Colvin's lectures on the Amazons, which he attended.

June

9 (Thurs) RB dines with Gustav Natorp.

18–20 He visits Jowett at Balliol.

July

This month Hiram Corson (1828–1911), Professor of English Literature at Cornell University and founder of the first known Browning club, comes to meet RB, who greets him with 'charming, chatty talk' rather than the 'high argument' for which Corson has been preparing himself. RB shows him the Old Yellow Book and translates the Latin arguments of the lawyers with 'rapid and close recasting of the thought in English, a rare gift even with the best Latin scholars'.

12 (Tues) He has been giving 'kind help' with Sidney Colvin's book on Landor (1881) in the English Men of Letters series. He likes Colvin's account of 'my dear provoking admirable unwise learned childish friend'.

15 RB has just read the poem *Dorothy, a Country Story*, an anonymously published work by Arthur Munby, and writes to ask the publisher, Charles Kegan Paul, to tell the author that it is 'literally years since I have admired and enjoyed a poem *so much*'. The exquisiteness of observation makes him think the author may be a woman, and if he is wrong this is the greater praise for 'a consummate male craftsman'. SB and Pen share his enthusiasm.

18   RB's good friend Dean Stanley dies. He attends the funeral in Westminster Abbey on 25.
27   RB dines with Natorp.
c. 28   RB and the journalist George Sala are among the Skirrows' guests at their end of season dinner (apparently a regular event) at the Ship Hotel, Greenwich.

August
8   (Mon) RB and SB set off from London for St Pierre de Chartreuse where, from 11, they stay at Hôtel Virard and go for long walks.
28   RB receives proofs of the first part of Furnivall's *A Bibliography of Robert Browning, from 1833 to 1881* (1881). 'It makes me feel as I look at the thing, as if I were dead and *begun* with, after half a century'. Further proofs reach him on 18 September.

September
16   (Fri) In a field near St Pierre d'Entremont – a hamlet seen by RB and SB on their mountain walks – a man, seemingly caught stealing potatoes, is killed and horribly mutilated. Around the time of the murder RB, out walking as usual, is wondering what it would be like to find a corpse in a field. 'I attribute no sort of supernaturalism to my fancy about the thing that was really about to take place' (to Eliza FitzGerald, 3 September 1882). 'By a law of association ... the peace and solitude readily called up the notion of what would most jar with them.'
18   RB and SB, having been delayed because the *juge d'instruction* from Grenoble is using the only mule to investigate the murder, leave St Pierre de Chartreuse for Chambéry.
19   At Chambéry they visit Rousseau's Les Charmettes before going on to Turin (20) and Venice, where, from 21, they again stay at Albergo dell'Universo.
23   They are introduced by the Layards to Countess Mocenigo at Palazzo Mocenigo and are shown Byron's rooms and desk.

October

28 (Fri) First meeting of the Browning Society at University College, London. The founders are Furnivall and Emily Hickey. (A reprint of the *Essay on Shelley* is the first publication of the Society.)

November

1 (Wed) RB and SB travel from Venice to Turin and from there to Mâcon (2), Paris (3) and London (4). During their absence the garden at 19 Warwick Crescent has been being put in order with plants and expert assistance from Eliza FitzGerald.

8 FitzGerald, whose mentally ill son Robert died on 28 October, comes for the 'quietest of dinners' with RB and SB.

14 RB sits to W.P. Frith for his large picture of notables at 'The Private View of the Royal Academy Exhibition'.

24 RB has written 'a poem or two ... which may or may not go into a new volume of Idyls' (which *The Athenaeum* has suggested is imminent). The poems are probably among those for *Jocoseria*.

December

8 (Thurs) RB sees R.H. Horne.

13 He hears Lowell speak in memory of Dean Stanley at the Chapter House, Westminster Abbey.

19 He pays £1. 5s. for solitaires, and on 21 £3. 5s. for a bracelet, for 'A' (very probably Alexandra Orr).

c. 31 RB speaks to Lowell and the painter James McNeill Whistler, among others, at the Grosvenor Gallery.

1882

RB's 'Terse Verse' – an impromptu which finds rhymes for the birthplaces of Thomas and Jane Carlyle, Ecclefechan and Craigenputtock, to entertain AT – may date from this year.

January

12   (Thurs) Pen, after a Christmas visit, returns briefly to Dinant before going to Paris, where he studies for two months with Auguste Rodin. By now Pen is, in RB's opinion as expressed to George Barrett on 2 May, a 'dear, good and absolutely satisfactory fellow'.

March

RB, with Herbert Spencer, T.H. Huxley, and AT, is among the signatories of a protest against the Submarine Railway Company's proposed Channel Tunnel. The tunnel would expose Britain to 'military dangers and liabilities'.

April

15   (Sat) RB dines with Gustav Natorp.
25   He assures Furnivall that he has never read Kant, Schelling, or Hegel.

May

 2   (Mon) RB is concerned, he tells George Barrett, about the fate of the many letters of EBB which he owns and has (making an exception for those used by Horne in 1873–4) so far protected from publication. RB is about to be seventy and must soon decide what needs to be destroyed. He and the Barretts are united in wanting to keep some secrets, principally the extent of EBB's involvement in spiritualism and dependence on morphine. But he has no access to the letters to her sisters, and is not encouraged by George to burn what he does have.

 7   RB's seventieth birthday. Furnivall presents him, on behalf of the Browning Society, with a set of RB's works, bound in green morocco, in an oak case decorated with bells, pomegranates and other designs inspired by the poems.

Possibly in May RB writes 'Never the Time and the Place' (*Jocoseria*).

Milsand visits RB (until 31). RB also sees Bronson during her visit to London.

June

13 (Tues) – 15 He is in Oxford, where on 14 he is awarded an honorary DCL. During the ceremony in the Sheldonian Theatre a red cotton nightcap is lowered onto his head from the gallery by an undergraduate. (The culprit is pardoned by the authorities on RB's intervention.)

Corson, in London to read a paper to the Browning Society on 'The Idea of Personality' in RB's poetry, comes to Warwick Crescent with his wife. RB's conversation at lunch strikes him as that of 'a person utterly free ... of self-conscious and intellectual vanity'.

August

1 (Tues) RB and SB set off from London for St Pierre de Chartreuse, where from *c*. 7 they again stay at Hôtel Virard. They learn that the owner of the field at St Pierre d'Entremont, accused of the murder (see September 1881), committed suicide, still swearing that the victim's companions had killed him.

15 James Darmesteter's French account and translation of 'Hervé Riel' appears in *Le Parlement*. Furnivall sends it to RB, who has read it by 22, is generally approving, and points out a few misunderstandings of English idiom.

RB writes 'Donald' (*Jocoseria*). He probably writes at least some of the other poems for the volume in St Pierre or soon after his return to London in October.

September

At St Pierre he has been reading mainly *The Iliad* and the newspapers, where he follows Sir Garnet Wolseley's expedition to suppress an Egyptian army rebellion. He 'rejoices at' Wolseley's victory of 13 (Wed).

18 RB and SB leave St Pierre for Chambéry and (19) Turin They intend to go to Vicenza and Venice but their plans are disrupted by floods. RB also suffers acutely from what he takes for rheumatism but his doctor diagnoses as liver trouble. They travel back from Bologna, probably via Paris, to arrive in London *c*. 1 October.

October
Pen has taken a studio in Paris for six months.

November
The extended version of the epilogue to *Idyls (II)* written in Edith Bronson's album in October 1880 is published in *The Century Magazine*. RB is angered both by the breach of privacy and because he feels that the lines spoil the effect of the original poem.

1   (Wed) RB dines with Anthony Trollope at the Garrick. Trollope suffers a disabling stroke the following day.

27–8   RB visits Sidney Colvin in Cambridge.

December
4   (Mon) RB and SB attend the opening by the Queen of the new Law Courts in the Strand.

6   Trollope dies. On 9 RB goes to the funeral at Kensal Green Cemetery.

17   RB and other members of the Cosmopolitan Club are at a dinner for Sir Garnet Wolseley, recently created Lord Wolseley in honour of his military success in Egypt.

22   'Jochanan Hakkadosh' (*Jocoseria*) is completed.

1883

January
9   (Tues) The manuscript of *Jocoseria* is sent to press. It is 'a collection of things gravish and gayish', an 'Olla Podrida', RB tells Furnivall. At this stage it contains eleven poems but, probably later this month, RB decides to omit 'Gerousios Oinos', thus avoiding potential rows with the contemporary poets whose thin wine, the poem has it, has succeeded to the old poets' 'good tipple'.

23   He buys a Hebrew Grammar.

During the Easter Term *Strafford* is studied at the North London Collegiate School for Girls, probably in a version prepared by Emily Hickey. (Her edition, incorporating

some suggestions and revisions by RB, will be published in
1884.)

March

9   (Fri) *Jocoseria* is published by Smith, Elder at 5s. Reviews
are generous and it is reprinted twice, in 1883 and 1885.
RB puts the volume's popularity down to the influence
of the increasing number of Browning Societies.

17 FitzGerald has sought learned aid in her attempts to
understand several of the poems in *Jocoseria*. RB maintains vigorously that the poems themselves contain all
necessary explanations: 'poetry, if it is to deserve the
name, ought to create – or reanimate something – not
merely reproduce it from somebody else's book.'

April

RB reads J.A. Froude's edition of *Letters and Memorials of
Jane Welsh Carlyle* (1883).

17 (Tues) RB dates and signs EBB's Hebrew Bible.

26 He buys a *Jewish Family Bible* and *Student's Hebrew
Lexicon.*

May

2   (Wed) He goes to Oxford for a lunch at Balliol in
honour of the Prince of Wales, where he sits opposite
the Duke of Buckingham and Chandos.

Milsand stays with RB.

4   RB sends one of Pen's portraits of him for exhibition at
the Grosvenor Gallery.

5   He goes to the Royal Academy dinner and inspects
work by Pen, William Logsdail (whose picture of St
Mark's Square he particularly admires), Millais,
Leighton (off form, he feels) and others.

RB briefly visits Paris to see Pen and his recently completed
statue *Dryope Fascinated by Apollo in the Form of a Serpent*,
arriving by 26 and returning on 30.

June

At the beginning of the month RB stays with FitzGerald at
Shalstone.

11 (Mon) While taking tea with Leighton RB writes 'Classicality Applied to Tea-Dealing: a Fancy Inspired By Westbourne Grove', a slightly different version of the tea poem of February 1834. In the evening he dines with Natorp.

22 He sees Odo Russell, now Lord Ampthill.

24 and 30 He meets the American poet and Jewish rights activist Emma Lazarus (1849–87).

July

10 (Tues) Sir James Ingham having written Horace's *Satires* I.iii.1–3 in Felix Moscheles' album, RB adds, impromptu, his own translation ('On Singers'; see 13 December).

15 RB and Edmund Gosse examine the papers of Thomas Lovell Beddoes (1803–49), bequeathed to RB by Beddoes' friend Thomas Forbes Kelsall in October 1872.

'The Eagle' (*Ferishtah*) is possibly written about now.

August

Early in the month RB goes to see recently discovered manuscripts of the Book of Deuteronomy at the British Museum.

3 (Fri) Finding Moscheles at work in his studio on two cloud pieces, RB recites Shelley's 'The Cloud' to him and, in a letter of the following day, suggests appropriate mottoes from it.

13 RB and SB leave London and travel to Turin, Ivrea, and, after a long and difficult mule-ride on 22, Hotel Delapierre, Gressoney St Jean. Gressoney is quiet, cool, and almost unknown to the English. It is just under Monte Rosa, 'one huge white from crest to base'; 'a little rapid river – the Lys – runs in the mid valley, white like the glaciers that feed it'.

September

4 (Tues) Teena Rochfort-Smith, a young RB enthusiast, close friend and (unknown to RB) lover of Furnivall, dies of burns suffered when her dress caught fire. On 9

RB tells Furnivall (probably with a degree of exaggeration) that the poetry he is writing (*Ferishtah*) 'will be much influenced by this experience, I do not doubt'.

12   RB writes or completes the Prologue to *Ferishtah*. Between now and 20 (probably) he works on the *Ferishtah* poems 'The Melon-Seller', 'Shah Abbas', 'The Family', and 'The Sun'.

20   'Mihrab Shah' (*Ferishtah*) is finished up to line 130. By 23 'A Camel-Driver' is finished, apart from its lyric and some emendations in proof. RB then begins work on 'Two Camels', but does not complete it until 15 January 1884.

About now he meets, through FitzGerald, Emily Harris, London Jewish writer and charity-worker, with whom he corresponds frequently from the spring of 1884; she dedicates to him her novel *Benedictus* (1887).

October

1   (Tues) Having walked for seven hours from Gressoney to Pont St Martin on 30 September, RB and SB travel from there to Ivrea (1) and Vicenza (2). On 3 they move on to Venice, where they are accommodated by Katharine Bronson in Palazzo Giustiniani-Recanati, next to her Ca' Alvisi. Here they engage in social life, walk, and are taken about by Bronson's gondoliers. The only disappointment is that 'the exquisite little island of St Helena – all but one garden with a solitary church, two years ago' is now 'a treeless yard built over by an iron foundry – the most hideous object imaginable'.

9   RB and SB dine with the Layards.

At the end of the month RB, SB, Bronson and her daughter Edith nearly go to Athens, which RB has always wanted to see. But there is not enough time; while RB and SB would take the short crossing from Brindisi to Patras, Bronson's poor health and habit of travelling in comfort would mean that the party would have to sail all the way from Venice to Athens.

In Venice RB continues to write *Ferishtah*.

November
Early this month RB is at a dinner where the guests include several exiled or displaced royals, among them Don Carlos, claimant to the Spanish throne.

27   (Tues) RB's sonnet 'Goldoni' is written at the request of the committee for the erection of a statue of the dramatist. The poem is to be included in an album of tributes. Also this autumn RB is present at the unveiling of a commemorative tablet to Baldassare Galuppi on Burano.

28   RB writes, at Katharine Bronson's request, the sonnet 'Sighed Rawdon Brown: "Yes, I'm departing, Toni! ..."

December
1   (Sat) The Epilogue to *Ferishtah* is written or completed.

8   'Goldoni' is published in *The Pall Mall Gazette*.

8   RB and SB leave Venice. Bronson's hospitality has persuaded them to stay much longer than intended. They go to Basle and (11) Paris – visiting Pen who has been working here once more – and reach London on 13. Since one of the staff at 19 Warwick Crescent, Edwin Guilliam, is dying of diphtheria they stay (in her absence) at FitzGerald's house in Portland Place. (SB is able to return home on 18.)

13   RB's 'On Singers' is published in *The Pall Mall Gazette*.

17   RB goes to Hatfield House, Hertfordshire, to stay with Lord and Lady Salisbury and meet the Duke and Duchess of Albany. Others present include RB's friend Lord Carnarvon. He returns to Warwick Crescent on 21.

28   RB's 'Helen's Tower' (see 26 April 1870) is published in *The Pall Mall Gazette*.

1884

January
3   (Thurs) He refuses another request by students of St Andrews University to stand for their Lord Rectorship.

14   Katharine Bronson needs a plot for a *commedietta,* to be privately performed at Ca' Alvisi. RB outlines 'a reminiscence from a little sketch I read, years ago, in an Italian newspaper' in which a man and woman at an inn decide to play along with the landlord's belief that they are lovers; the acting brings out their real love for each other. At about the beginning of February Bronson sends RB her writing up of this scenario, which has not survived.

c. 15   RB takes up work on *Ferishtah* once more, having paused probably since the end of September 1883 (except for the Epilogue). After finishing 'Two Camels' he writes 'Cherries' on 15 and completes 'Plot-Culture' on 17. Soon afterwards follow 'A Pillar at Sebzevar' and 'A Bean-Stripe; Also, Apple-Eating' (up to line 364; the remaining lines are added at some point between now and September). The lyrics accompanying the poems are mostly written either now or later in the year.

23   RB visits Gustav Natorp.

February
RB's sonnet on Rawdon Brown appears in *The Century Magazine.*

March
 1   (Sat) RB sees Salvini's King Lear, followed probably by his Othello on 3 and his lead role in Soumet's *Gladiator* on 14.
13   RB lunches with Natorp.
29   Works by Pen are shown (until 1 April) at 11 Campden House Road Mews.

April
 5   (Sat) RB writes 'The Founder of the Feast', published in *The World* on 16.
14–20   He goes to Edinburgh where, on 17, honorary LLDs are conferred on him, AT (*in absentia*) and 121 other notables. He is surprised into making a brief speech.

Milsand stays at 19 Warwick Crescent.

22   Pen arrives in London and organises the moving of his statue *Dryope Fascinated* from the Royal Academy to the Grosvenor Gallery. According to Charles Hallé RB wept when the Grosvenor initially refused to take *Dryope* after its rejection by the Academy. (The Academy's treasurer, J.C. Horsley, objected to the statue's nudity. See 20–25 May 1885.)

26   RB includes in a letter to FitzGerald his limerick on Folkestone.

May

12   (Mon) RB writes 'The Names', published on 29 in *Shaksperean Show Book*. (The show, in the Royal Albert Hall, takes place on 29–31.)

24–26   He visits Jowett at Balliol.

SB is seriously ill with peritonitis.

June

25   (Wed) RB is at Hallam Tennyson's wedding to Audrey Boyle in Westminster Abbey. Houghton and Arnold are also among the guests.

28–30   He stays at Balliol again.

August

A coin of the Venetian Republic of 1848, sent to RB by Katharine Bronson, is attached to his watch-chain, 'the only other token of love there being my wife's ring'. He tells her that he loves the coin as EBB would have loved it – 'You know what she felt and wrote about United Italy'.

c. 15   (Fri) RB and SB leave London. On about 17 they reach Villa Berry, St Moritz, which has been rented by their friend Clara Bloomfield-Moore (who is called away to America at the beginning of September). Again they go for long mountain walks. They do not, this year, go on to Italy, initially because of quarantine regulations during an outbreak of cholera, and also because Katharine Bronson is away from home.

September

8   (Mon) RB sends the final proofs of *Ferishtah* to George Smith. A late addition is 'Not With My Soul, Love! ...' – the lyric to accompany 'Plot-Culture' – which possibly responds to Clara Bloomfield-Moore's words, as she left for America, on her 'Soul-love' for him.

October

1   (Wed) RB and SB leave St Moritz. They arrive in London on 3.

13   RB and Henry James are among Sidney Colvin's dinner-guests.

November

10   (Mon) Students at Glasgow University again wish to nominate RB for the Rectorship. He again refuses.

21   *Ferishtah's Fancies* is published by Smith, Elder at 5s. There are two further editions in 1885.

23   RB dines with Frederick and Nina Lehmann.

28   SB is present at the Browning Society production of *In a Balcony* at the Prince's Hall, Piccadilly. Another performance is given at the Century Club in Birmingham on 16 December.

December

10   (Wed) AT sends RB a copy of his *Becket*.

13   Charles J. Lyall sends RB a letter containing suggested corrections to Persian names in *Ferishtah*. Almost all of these are incorporated in the third edition in 1885.

19   Lawrence Barrett's production of RB's *A Blot*, with Barrett himself as Tresham, opens in Washington, DC, at the beginning of a tour continuing until May 1886.

1885

RB's 'Why I am a Liberal' is published in a book of the same name edited by Andrew Reid. Other contributors include Gladstone.

March

11   (Wed) RB calls on Fanny Kemble. Afterwards he meets Domett; they agree on the absurdity of Holman Hunt's *The Triumph of the Innocents.*

15   (Sun) In response to Gosse's request that RB nominate 'Four Poems, of moderate length, which represent their writer fairly' he chooses ('at a venture') 'Lyrical: *Saul* or *Abt Vogler.* Narrative: *A Forgiveness.* Dramatic: *Caliban on Setebos.* Idyllic (in the Greek sense): *Clive'.*

April

19   (Sun) RB dates his lines for the tomb of Levi Lincoln Thaxter, an American Browning reader and interpreter, first published in *Poet Lore* in August.

30   *A Blot* is produced in London for the Browning Society (repeated on 2 May). RB, who is at the first performance, concealed behind muslin curtains, contrasts the care taken with the performance by amateurs with 'the carelessness and worse of Macready'.

May

20   (Wed) – 25 Attacks on the nude in art in *The Times*, led by Horsley of the Royal Academy, fuel further RB's anger on Pen's behalf, channelled subsequently into the 'Parleying With Francis Furini' of 1887.

26   RB and SB dine with the Lowells.

June

16   (Tues) – 17 RB visits Jowett at Balliol.

RB receives 'a scrupulous account of his doings, and a handsome cheque' from Lawrence Barrett, still touring America with *A Blot.*

30   At a party given by Sir John Everett Millais RB meets the explorer Henry Morton Stanley.

July

1   (Wed) RB dines at the International Exhibition of Inventions at the Royal Albert Hall.

25   Possible date of RB's impromptu lines to greet the actress and theatre manager Marie Bancroft at a dinner at the Star and Garter, Richmond.

August

18   (Tues) RB and SB set off from London, via Basle and (19) Pont St Martin, for Gressoney St Jean (20), where again they stay at Hôtel Delapierre. Gressoney remains a place of extreme beauty and solitariness; 'St Moritz is Cheapside by comparison'.

September

7   (Mon) RB gives Furnivall permission to 'biographize about both of us' (see November), while saying that he knows little of EBB's earlier life and is forced to stay silent about what little he does know. In the same letter he tells Furnivall that he is writing a new poem, presumably *Parleyings*. Between now and the end of the year, probably, he produces the Parleyings with Bernard de Mandeville, Daniel Bartoli, Christopher Smart and Gerard de Lairesse, and 'Fust and his Friends: an Epilogue'.

10   RB and SB go to see the remains of houses in Gressoney which were destroyed, with some loss of life, in an avalanche eight months earlier.

29   They move on to Palazzo Giustiniani-Recanati, Venice. Social life is quieter than in 1883 because Katharine Bronson is in mourning following the death of her husband in March. RB goes often, however, to Venetian-dialect plays (including some Goldoni) at the Teatro Goldoni, following 'the voluble and by no means easy dialogue with a foreigner's difficulty – though I can read Venetian with tolerable ease'. He admires the versatile playing of Emilio Zago (1852–1929). Pen, having arrived and hired a studio at the end of September, is also present. In Italy for the first time since 1861, he revives old times with Ferdinando Romagnoli, still cook with an American family in Venice.

October

18   (Sun) At Ca' Alvisi RB reads, to a group including the Storys, Curtises, and Layards, 'Hervé Riel', 'Andrea del Sarto', 'Youth and Art', 'A Toccata of Galuppi's', 'Incident of the French Camp', and 'The Statue and the Bust'.

November

Early this month RB's negotiations for the purchase of Palazzo Manzoni in Venice appear to be concluded. (He wants the palace for Pen, who has developed a great enthusiasm for Venice, and as a 'capital retreat' for his own last years.) But the owner Marchese Montecuccoli and his lawyers cause various delays and difficulties. Eventually RB withdraws from the resulting law-suit – paying, early in 1887, costs of £12. 7s. as well as his own lawyer's fee of £16.2s.6d. – when Pen learns of structural faults in the building.

4   (Wed) At the Curtises' apartment in Palazzo Barbaro RB reads 'The Italian in England', 'Home-Thoughts, from Abroad', 'Date and Dabitur', and either 'Master Hugues of Saxe-Gotha' or 'A Toccata of Galuppi's'.

17   RB and SB are the guests of the Spanish pretender Don Carlos.

19   Furnivall has sent proofs of his articles on the Brownings for *Celebrities of the Century*, ed. Lloyd C. Sanders (1887). RB is generally approving but asks him to remove a remark critical of Orr's *Handbook* (which Furnivall regards as too long and too expensive).

23   RB and SB leave Venice. They reach London on 25.

December

5   (Sat) RB is in Cambridge to see Aeschylus' *Eumenides* performed in Greek at the Theatre Royal with music by Charles Villiers Stanford. He returns to London on 8.

7   RB is elected Honorary President of the University of Edinburgh for 1886–7. He is willing at last to accept such an honour because no duties whatsoever are involved.

8   RB refuses the presidency of the Shelley Society which Furnivall is forming. Shelley does not need a society as RB himself had; moreover there is a painful contrast between what he now feels about Shelley and what he felt sixty years ago.

8   SB finds in 'an evening paper' that AT has dedicated *Tiresias and Other Poems* 'To My Good friend' RB. AT sends a copy soon afterwards.

1886

January

RB has refused a request to publish a poem in the New York *Independent*. He also rejects, probably this year, a £400 offer for a poem for a Boston magazine, explaining to the editor that if people choose to buy his books they evidently want to read his work, while in a magazine he would be 'an uninvited guest'. EBB by contrast 'liked it; she liked to be with the others'.

6   (Wed) 'Epps' is written.

20 RB buys a copy of George Bubb Dodington's *Diary* (1784), a source for the Parleying with Dodington which he writes within the next few months. (He first read the diary probably in the 1830s.)

February

13 (Sat) He lunches with Natorp.

March

25 (Thurs) He attends a concert given by the pianist and composer Agnes Zimmerman at the Prince's Hall, Piccadilly.

This month the 'Parleying With Charles Avison' is probably written.

April

RB is trying, for the good of his health, to avoid non-imperative visiting, but still manages a good number of engagements.

7 (Wed) He is at dinner with Joachim.
8 He dines, with others including the French ambassador William-Henry Waddington, at 50 Albermarle Street with the publisher John Murray III. Here he sees the manuscript of *Childe Harold's Pilgrimage*, Canto III, noting that 'the corrections were infinite and, so far as I could observe, all much for the better', and the fireplace in which Byron's memoirs were burnt.

May
7 (Fri) RB, on his seventy-fourth birthday, is a guest of honour at the Shelley Society's performance of Shelley's *The Cenci*, with Alma Murray as Beatrice, at the Grand Theatre, Islington. Lowell and George Meredith are also present.
13 (Thurs) RB has just read *Baldwin: Being Dialogues on Views and Aspirations* (1886) by Vernon Lee (Violet Paget, 1856–1935), whom he mentions in 'Apprehensiveness' (*Asolando*).
26 He dines with Mary (Mrs Humphry) Ward.

June
Bronson, visiting London, sees RB.
29 (Tues) RB goes to Balliol for a visit which includes social occasions connected with the end of Jowett's term as Vice Chancellor of the university and, on 30, a Commemoration at the Sheldonian Theatre in which a degree is conferred on Oliver Wendell Holmes, whom he has recently met several times. Lowell also comes to Oxford.
Late in the month SB is for a time dangerously ill and is still convalescent in July–August. As a result RB and SB decide not to go abroad this summer.

July
c. 13 (Tues) RB, Hardy, and Wilde dine with the Skirrows.

August
13 (Fri) RB and SB arrive in Llangollen, where they stay at the Hand Hotel. This has been arranged by Sir

Theodore and Lady (Helen Faucit) Martin, who live nearby at Bryntysilio and see them often during their visit. By the end of the month SB largely recovers her strength and joins RB on several-hour walks.

September

2   (Thurs) RB and SB visit Chester and are guided round 'the fine old picturesque place' by Sir Theodore Martin.

4   Death of RB's close friend Joseph Milsand at his house in Villers-la-Faye near Beaune. Soon afterwards RB writes 'Apollo and the Fates: a Prologue' (*Parleyings*).

30 RB dates as finished the 'Parleying With Francis Furini'. (Lines 601–7 accompanied Pen's painting of Joan of Arc (nude) with the kingfisher, attacked by Horsley, in 1886.) Work on *Parleyings* is largely complete.

October

5   (Tues) – 7 RB reads, likes, and makes minor revisions in Arthur Symons' *Introduction to the Study of Browning* (1886).

20 RB and SB return to London.

November

24 RB again states to John H. Ingram that he will provide no information to biographers of EBB. He was prepared only to verify dates for Mrs Richmond Ritchie's article in *DNB*. But now 'it *may* happen, as adverse things will, that I shall myself, on compulsion, endeavour as briefly as possible to substitute fact for fiction' with the help of the many documents he possesses.

RB possibly attends the Cambridge Greek play.

December

This month 'Spring Song' (lines 426–34 of the 'Parleying With Gerard de Lairesse') is published in *The New Amphion*, 'The Book of the Edinburgh University Union Fancy Fair'. He suffers from 'spasmodic asthma'.

4   (Sat) *Parleyings* has gone to press; the last corrected proofs are sent to George Smith on 25.

Early in the month RB reads Edward Dowden's *The Life of Percy Bysshe Shelley* (1886) 'with such an increasing irritation at the poor silly boy, – and not much respect for his biographer, – otherwise my friend and well-wisher, – that I hope to never again hear a word for or against Shelley'.

16   RB receives a copy of 'Locksley Hall Sixty Years After' from AT.

21   A Browning Society production of *Strafford* is given at the Strand Theatre. RB doubts that the play can succeed without a Strafford of Macready's quality.

1887

January

About now RB spends 'more than a week' destroying letters, among them those he sent his family up to the death of his father in 1866.

28   (Fri) *Parleyings With Certain People of Importance in their Day* is published by Smith, Elder at 10s. The volume is dedicated to the memory of Milsand. Most reviews are unenthusiastic; the author, 'who often amuses himself by writing in a cipher to which he alone has the key, has seldom propounded to his disciples a more hopeless puzzle' (*The Saturday Review*, 26 February). In America *Parleyings* is published by Houghton Mifflin, whose agreement with RB (the volume carries his statement that they are 'the authorised publishers for the United States') ends many years of difficult dealings with other American publishers.

February

19   (Sat) A version of RB's letter to W. Hamlet Smith (sent on 10), dismissing hostile criticism as the hissing of geese, is published in *The Pall Mall Gazette*.

March

At the end of the month RB dines with Joseph Joachim and Clara Schumann and is at a house where she gives a private performance.

April

1 (Fri) RB dines at G.O. Trevelyan's.
2 He is at the Anglo-Jewish exhibition at the Royal Albert Hall. (He is a member of the General Committee and has lent two Hebrew Bibles.)
3 He lunches with Jowett and the Speaker of the House of Commons, Arthur Wellesley Peel.

June

c. 2 (Thurs) The Prince of Wales approaches RB to write 'a poem to be set to music by [Sir Arthur] Sullivan on the occasion of the Queen's laying the first stone of the Imperial Institute'; AT at first apparently 'shirked Laureate-duty' but in the event 'tacked a couple of verses on to his "Secular Ode"' (RB tells Bronson on 20).
3 RB pays £5000 for his new house, 29 De Vere Gardens, Kensington. For several years Warwick Crescent has been under threat of demolition as a result of railway-building plans under the Regents Park Bill; in fact the railway will be abandoned and the old house stand until 1960.
12 or 19 Hardy finds RB uncharacteristically sleepy at Mrs Procter's. 'In telling a story [he] would break off, forgetting what he was going to say.'
15 He has read and expresses enthusiasm for Sidney Colvin's *Keats* (1887) in the English Men of Letters series.
17 RB and SB move to 29 De Vere Gardens. Henry James is already living at no. 34.
21–23 RB visits Jowett at Balliol. He is, Hardy reports on 26, 'galled' that he – and many others eminent in art and science – has not been been invited to the Queen's Jubilee ceremony at Westminster Abbey.

July

23 (Sat) – 24 RB and SB travel from London to Chur and St Moritz, where they are again Clara Bloomfield-Moore's guests at Villa Berry.

August
RB is delighted to hear that Fannie Coddington has accepted Pen's proposal of marriage. (They met again in July, having known each other years before – the first proposal was rejected in 1873.) RB assures his son that she 'has every requisite to make you happy and successful' and 'has spoken to me with the greatest frankness and generosity of the means she will have to contributing to your support'. He will provide £300 a year and there will also be profits from the sale of Pen's works.

September
12 (Mon) RB and SB leave St Moritz for Basle (13), Amiens (14) and London (15).

October
 1 (Sat) RB and SB go to Hawkwell, near Pembury in Kent, where on 14 Pen Browning marries Fannie Coddington. The couple go to Venice and then, after a week in London, sail for New York on 5 November.
George Smith and RB begin to discuss the collected edition which will become *1888–9*. It is decided by late December that it will consist of fifteen or sixteen volumes, combining the six volumes of *1868* with RB's subsequent publications.

November
 2 (Wed) Alfred Domett dies. On 17 RB, dining at the Lehmanns', says that Domett was 'a man who always impressed me as capable of greater things than he achieved'.
12 RB tells George Smith that he has changed his mind about adding headnotes (as suggested by Furnivall) to the collected edition; he prefers to let the poems stand alone, independent of the poet's 'life and habits'. He continues to change his mind, however, finally deciding against notes only in December.
26 RB is sorry not to be in Cambridge for the Greek Play, for which Stanford has composed the music. But he

'dreaded the long hot business, – not to speak of the hospitalities of next day'.

RB reads, and suggests amendments in, Felix Moscheles' translation of Felix Mendelssohn's letters to Moscheles' parents. On 30 RB provides, for inclusion in this work, a translation ('Hail to the man who upward strives ...') of Karl Klingeman's poem on Ignaz Moscheles.

Natorp is working on a low-relief head of RB which will be shown at the Royal Academy in 1888. Sittings continue through December and January. RB continues much in the society of artists including Leighton and Alma-Tadema.

December

17 (Sat) He hears Leighton deliver 'a learned and instructive discourse' at the annual Royal Academy prize-giving ceremony. He speaks to Tadema and Luke Fildes.

18 (Sun) RB composes lines for the window celebrating the Queen's Jubilee in St Margaret's Church, Westminster, requested on 17 by Archdeacon Frederick Farrar and published in *The Pall Mall Gazette* on 4 January 1888.

22 RB dines with a group including Lord Wolseley and the high court judge and writer Sir James FitzJames Stephen, whom RB often sees.

'Rosny' (*Asolando*) may date from late this month, as may the *Asolando* 'Bad Dreams' sequence.

1888

January

13 (Fri) RB has finished correcting the six *1868* volumes for *1888–9*.

He is ill with rheumatic pain and coughing and still confined to his room when Henry James visits on 19.

23 Pen cables from America to tell RB and SB that Fannie has miscarried.

February

4 (Sat) In the *Athenaeum* Ingram (mistakenly) defends the 'facts' he has published about EBB – about her date

and place of birth for instance – which RB has already stated to be inaccurate.

8   By now RB has recovered sufficiently to begin to go back into society.

11 In the *Athenaeum* he replies to Ingram, stating that he has indisputable sources – documents furnished by George Barrett – for the correct facts about EBB.

24 RB receives proofs of the first volume of *1888–9*; he decides to correct obvious faults of 'expression, versification and construction' in *Pauline*. The proofs are returned to Smith on 7 March.

March

RB is pleased at the political success of Joseph Chamberlain, leader of the Unionist Liberals opposed to Gladstone on the issue of Irish Home Rule. RB's friendship with Gladstone has effectively ended (but see 14 May).

Anne Procter (1799–1888) dies. RB's Sunday afternoon visits to her continued after the death of Bryan Waller Procter in 1874.

15 (Thurs) RB is present when a performance of *A Blot*, arranged by the Browning Society, is given at the Olympic Theatre with Alma Murray as Mildred. Around this time he toys with the idea of writing a new tragedy.

17 RB and SB are at a party given by Professor Flower of the Zoological Gardens at the South Kensington Museum.

c. 20 Pen and Fannie arrive in London. They go to Venice at about the beginning of April.

April

RB attends exhibitions of work by Leighton, Prinsep, Fildes, and others.

He sees Ruskin.

23 (Mon) Pen is elected to the Athenaeum.

27 The sixteen volumes of RB's collected *Poetical Works* appear between now and July 1889 (price 5s. per volume or £4 the set).

May

He sees the Layards several times.

Hardy sends RB his *Wessex Tales*.

Early in the month RB is at the Royal Academy Exhibition, where he admires the medallion of himself by Natorp and paintings by Sargent, Leader, and Carolus Duran but finds those by Poynter 'dreadful – vulgar to the last degree'.

6   (Sun) RB sends George Smith corrections for the remaining volumes of *1888–9* (except for volume 13, to follow on 30 May). Proof correction continues until 5 June 1889 and he also goes on collecting errata from the volumes as they are printed.

7   Eliza FitzGerald's birthday gift to RB is a copy of *Coryats Crudities*.

14   RB is the guest of John Murray at 50 Albermarle Street. He sits next to Gladstone 'to my discomfiture' but finds, he writes to Pen and Fannie, that 'nobody could be more agreeable'.

June

10   (Sun) Allingham visits De Vere Gardens. RB talks about Darwin – 'whatever his merits as an investigator, his philosophy was of little or no importance' – and about his deep sense of the honour done him by actors' performances of his plays, given free, for the Browning Society.

17   RB dines with George and Katherine Boughton and Ada Rehan, the American actress who has been playing recently in *The Taming of the Shrew*.

19–23   He makes his annual visit to Jowett at Balliol for Commemoration on 20 and a dinner on the occasion of the Marquis of Landsowne becoming Viceroy of India on 22. Oxford carries perpetual reminders of 'the fleeting state of mortal things', he writes to Eliza FitzGerald on the day of his return.

July

At the end of the month RB receives from Gosse a copy of his new *Life of William Congreve*. Congreve's mother's name was Browning, and Gosse has suggested a possible link.

August

13   (Mon) RB and SB leave London. On 16 they join Pen and Fannie at Primiero in the Tyrol, staying at Albergo Gilli.

30   RB sends Bronson the first version of 'White Witchcraft' (*Asolando*).

September

At the beginning of the month Pen completes his purchase of Palazzo Rezzonico on the Grand Canal in Venice.

4   (Tues) RB and SB visit San Martino di Castrozza, a former monastery converted into a hotel and 'surrounded by wonderful mountains'. Here RB comes across acquaintances including the royal surgeon Sir James Paget (1814–99).

12   RB and SB move on to Venice, where they are accommodated for nearly three months by Katharine Bronson (this time in Ca' Alvisi itself rather than the Giustiniani-Recanati). The weather is fine and RB enjoys long walks on the Lido and watching and advising on Pen's expensive refurbishment of Palazzo Rezzonico. At some point RB reads, in Giuseppe Tassini's *Curiosità veneziane* (1863), the legend used in 'Ponte dell'Angelo, Venice'. He perhaps begins work on this poem soon afterwards. The other *Asolando* poems 'The Pope and the Net' and 'The Bean-Feast' may also be written around now.

December

11   (Tues) RB and SB travel to Basle and on 12–13 to Calais, arriving in London on 14.

25   RB tells the Skirrows that Fannie has 'again had a disappointment' – a second miscarriage?

1889

January

9   (Wed) RB completes 'Ponte dell'Angelo, Venice'.

To avoid being made ill by the contrast in climate between Venice and London RB decides to refuse evening invitations until the end of the month. He feels obliged, however, to agree to be present on 24 at the Lord Mayor's farewell dinner for the American ambassador, Edward Phelps.

21   RB is still worrying about the future of the hundreds of EBB letters he owns and cannot bring himself to destroy. Conceivably he would be prepared to present the correspondence on 'literature, politics, theology, descriptions of persons and things', but more intimate matters would be seized on and distorted by gossips. Her letters to him, he tells George Barrett, are 'immeasurably superior to any composition of the same kind I have any experience of'.

February

4   (Mon) RB dines with Natorp.

14   Possible date for 'Reverie' (*Asolando*).

March

3   (Sun) RB dines with George Boughton and talks with John Singer Sargent. At this time he calls on or dines with other artists including Natorp and Moscheles, who is working on the painting for which RB writes – varying lines suggested by Moscheles himself – the first version of 'The Isle's Enchantress'. The second, published version is finished by 7.

5   RB dines with Frederick Locker (afterwards Locker-Lampson) at Lady Thurston's; on 9 and 14 he sees the Layards at friends' houses; on 13 he dines with Lady Airlie and Lord and Lady Dufferin. During this busy season he also finds time to see his friends the Skirrows.

10   RB writes to Furnivall in the hope that he will be able to obtain work from the editor of *The Academy* for Francis Thompson, 'a young Poet of my acquaintance, author of some exceptionally good poems'.

24   He dines with Natorp, still one of the friends he sees most frequently.

26   'The Isle's Enchantress' is published in *The Pall Mall Gazette*.

27   He is at a morning gathering at Leighton's with Joseph Joachim (who probably provides music).

The chapel which is being designed for the Palazzo Rezzonico will be dedicated to the memory of EBB, whom Fannie 'from her girlhood has all but worshipped' according to RB. There will be a copy in letters of gold of the words inscribed on Casa Guidi and a statue of their author, Tommaseo.

April

1   (Mon) – 6 Pen's portrait of his father is to be seen, as RB proudly informs his friends, at 29 De Vere Gardens.

7   RB dines at Rudolf Lehmann's with, among others, Boughton and probably Joachim. Reluctantly, RB agrees to be recorded on a (recently developed) Edison wax cylinder. He starts to recite 'How They Brought the Good News from Ghent to Aix', breaks off in the fourth line, and declares 'I forget it ... I'm most terribly sorry but I can't remember my own verses.'

23   'Beatrice Signorini' (*Asolando*) is completed.

May

7   (Tues) RB is at Moscheles' studio. Over the next few days they discuss whether a painting Moscheles is engaged on would work as an illustration for Landor's *Gebir*, Book Five.

Pen and, more extensively, Fannie, visit RB and SB in London (until 2 June).

During the spring and summer RB sends Smith corrections to volumes 1–10 of *1888–9*. (He will not live to supply those for volumes 11–16.) These will be incorporated in the new edition of January 1890 (dated 1889).

June

1   (Sat) – 4 RB goes to Cambridge as the guest of the Master of Trinity College, Henry Butler. He is photographed by Eveleen Myers. One afternoon in the

Fellows' Garden at Trinity he talks to Edmund Gosse, with an unusual degree of intimacy, for two hours. He confesses to the 'long-drawn desolateness' of his unpopular or unnoticed 'early and middle life as a literary man' and tells 'stories of early loves and hatreds, Italian memories of the forties, stories with names in them that meant nothing to his ignorant listener'.

c. 10   At the Herkomer Theatre at Bushey in Hertfordshire RB is 'bored to extinction' by Hubert von Herkomer's *An Idyl.*

c. 10–15   RB dines at Sir Henry Thompson's with guests including the Layards, and on 18 with John Duke Coleridge (Lord Chief Justice since 1880).

25   RB goes to Balliol until 2 July. He is there for Commemoration and, on 1 July, the 'Gaudy' for the Provost and Fellows of Eton. There is more time than usual to be alone with Jowett.

'Muckle-Mouth Meg' (*Asolando*) is written in late June or early July.

July

6   (Sat) RB is among the guests (who include Gladstone, Millais, and the Prince of Wales) at Lord Rosebery's dinner for the Shah of Persia. He converses briefly with him in French, and agrees to give him one of his books.

8   RB comes upon an 1861 passage in Edward FitzGerald's posthumously published *Letters and Literary Remains* (1889) declaring that 'Mrs Browning's Death is rather a relief to me, I must say: no more Aurora Leighs, thank God! A woman of real Genius, I know' but women would do better to 'mind the Kitchen and their Children; and perhaps the Poor ...' The first of these remarks moves RB to immediate and extreme fury. He composes 'To Edward Fitzgerald' and sends it that day to *The Athenaeum*. On 9 he writes to Norman MacColl, one of the editors, that if the sentiment expressed in the poem 'is discordant with the

general tone of the poetry in your columns' he should send it back 'for publication elsewhere'. Possibly on 11 RB sends a telegram asking for the piece to be withdrawn but (tradition has it) MacColl deliberately fails to read the message until it is too late. The poem is published in *The Athenaeum* on 13. Aldis Wright, editor of the FitzGerald volume, apologises in *The Athenaeum* on 20 for having neglected to remove the offending remark (while privately expressing anger at the viciousness of RB's attack). In several letters to family and friends RB vigorously defends his conduct; had he stayed silent, it might have been said that he was 'placable' because in another letter FitzGerald calls him 'a great man', or have been explained in terms of 'the many falsehoods told about me, – of a gossiping kind'.

21 RB writes to Emily Tennyson. He has heard that his 'rough verses' ('To Edward Fitzgerald') have grieved her and perhaps AT, who was a friend of FitzGerald. He explains his position in some detail: 'I am unable to regret what I did, – bitterly as I regret having been compelled to do it.' Writing this letter has tested his 'power of self-control'.

As a result of the FitzGerald affair RB is 'quite ill', SB tells Pen.

August

5 (Tues) RB sends greetings to AT on the eve of his eightieth birthday, assuring him of unswerving affection and esteem. Writing to Pen on 16 he expresses relief – in view of the attack on FitzGerald – that the Laureate has replied (11) with similar pledges.

8 RB expresses uncertainty to Bronson as to whether he will travel as far as Italy this year; the prospect of the journey is becoming more daunting in 'the laziness of age'. Soon afterwards, however, persuaded by Bronson and by Pen, he makes up his mind to come.

21 RB, in a letter to John T. Nettleship, revises lines 87–103 of the 'Parleying With Christopher Smart'.

22 He meets Arthur Symons.
27 In a letter to Edward Berdoe he agrees to support an
    anti-vivisectionist hospital. Possibly the anti-vivisec-
    tionist 'Arcades Ambo' (*Asolando*) is written around
    now.
29–30 RB and SB travel, by way of Basle, to Milan, where
    they spend two nights at the Hôtel de France.

September
 1 (Sun) RB and SB go on to Brescia and then Verona (2),
    Castelfranco (3) and Asolo (4), where they stay at the
    house of Nina Tabacchi, near Bronson's recently
    purchased La Mura. From the loggia of La Mura,
    Bronson records, RB often points out to other visitors
    sites he 'kept clear in his mind while writing *Sordello*
    and *Pippa Passes'*.
RB, with SB and Bronson, goes to performances by a
theatre troupe in the former palace of Queen Caterina
Cornaro.

October
Early in the month Pen visits RB and SB in Asolo.
RB opens negotiations to buy a plot of land in Asolo, once
part of Queen Caterina's pleasure-garden, and transform a
roofless building on it into 'Pippa's Tower'. He is supported
by the mayor of Asolo, opposed and then aided by Count
Loredano, a local lawyer.
RB and SB walk every morning and drive with Bronson
every afternoon, discovering new routes and views. They
drive several times to the tower of San Zenone where
Alberico and his family died (see *Sordello* V. 777–93) and buy
from a peasant six iron arrow-heads 'certainly of that time'
which have been dug up there. They also often drive to
Bassano, where RB enjoys visiting the small museum. On
the way back, on one occasion, he conceives 'The Lady and
the Painter' (*Asolando*), suggested, he tells Bronson, by 'the
birds twittering in the trees'. There is also a longer excursion to Nove and Marostica. In the evenings RB plays
Bronson's spinet and often reads aloud, sometimes from

his own work, more often from Shelley, Keats, Coleridge, and Tennyson. The only disadvantages of Asolo are some bad weather and cold accommodation.

15 (Tues) RB sends the manuscript of *Asolando* to Smith, Elder. 'Some few' of the poems have been written, and all of them 'supervised, in the comfort of your presence' (Dedication to Bronson dated 15) or at least in Asolo. The 'some few' probably include 'Inapprehensiveness' (early October?) and 'Dubiety' and possibly 'Flute-Music, With an Accompaniment'. The Epilogue seems likely also to date from this time.

The Storys come to Asolo. Just before they leave RB says to Story 'We have been friends for forty years – aye – more than forty years – and with never a break'.

31 RB and SB arrive in Venice to stay at Palazzo Rezzonico.

November
RB reads the third volume of Bronson's copy of Carlo Gozzi's *Memorie inutili* (1796–7); in Asolo he found the first two volumes 'insufferably tiresome and disgusting'.

2 (Sat) Hiram Corson visits RB. Over the next few days he sees him several times. They walk about Venice with RB pointing out things of interest and Corson finds it physically difficult to keep up with him. On the morning of 7, a few hours before Corson and his wife are leaving, he comes to their hotel and talks to them about Asolo, Pisa, EBB, his parents, paintings, Shakespeare, and Shelley, whose 'grander' features he still admires.

14 RB and Pen are photographed on the steps of the Rezzonico by Evelyn Barclay, a guest at the palace whose diary will record details of RB's illness and death.

Until late November RB leads a very active life, frequently seeing Katharine Bronson (back at Ca' Alvisi from early November), walking on the Lido, going to dinner-parties and tea-parties, and reading from *Asolando* – in the proofs of which he makes final revisions – and other works. (On 19 he reads and recites for two hours at the Curtises' apartment in Palazzo Barbaro.) About now he reads 'One who never turned his back ...', from the epilogue to *Asolando*, to SB and Fannie and tells them 'It almost looks like bragging to say this, and as if I ought to cancel it; but it's the simple truth; and as it's true, it shall stand'.

21   He develops a bad cough and is short of breath. He is suffering from bronchitis and a failing heart but believes at first that his symptoms denote liver problems and asthma.

24   Godfrey D. Giles, Evelyn Barclay's future husband, makes a pencil sketch of RB, who writes beneath it 'Here I'm gazing, wide awake,/Robert Browning, no mistake!'

27   RB dines with the Layards and a German admiral but has to come home early.

28   He goes to a production of Bizet's *Carmen*. He almost faints on the way up the Rezzonico stairs to his room. Dr Cini is called. The patient refuses to stay in bed.

December

1   (Sun) RB is confined to bed. He is cared for by Pen, Fannie, Evelyn Barclay, and Margherita Fiori, a Venetian nurse.

11   By now he is often delirious but has clear moments.

12   RB's *Asolando: Fancies and Facts* is published by Smith, Elder (dated 1890) at 5s. In the morning Fannie shows RB an advance copy. He looks at 'two different things he wanted to see'. At 5.00 p.m. he tells Margherita Fiori that he knows he is dying. At 6.30 Pen reads him a telegram from George Smith telling of the favourable reviews and good sales of *Asolando*. RB replies 'How gratifying' (according to Pen's letter to Bronson) or 'More than satisfied. I am dying. My dear boy. My dear boy' (according to the diary of Evelyn Barclay). He loses consciousness by about 8.00 and dies at 10.00.

13   Alexandra Orr arrives in Venice.

14 Pen learns that it is impossible for his father to be buried with EBB in the Protestant Cemetery in Florence. He accepts the Dean of Westminster's offer, telegraphed by George Smith after an interview with the Dean, of a place in the Abbey.

15 After a service at the Rezzonico, where mourners include Orr, Bronson, the Layards, the Curtises, the English and French consuls, and Venetian officials, the coffin is moved, on a black-and-gold barge followed by gondolas, to the cemetery island of San Michele, and then, between 17 and 20, transferred to London by train.

18 *Asolando* goes into second and third printings; a fourth follows on 23, a fifth on 30, and three more in 1890.

31 RB is buried, near Chaucer and Spenser, in Westminster Abbey. The pall-bearers include Jowett, Leighton, Hallam Tennyson, and George Smith (who has been in charge of the funeral arrangements). The choir sings a setting of lines from EBB's 'The Sleep' ('What would we give our beloved? ...'), which RB read at her funeral in 1861. Among the many notables present are Henry James, Gosse, Burne-Jones, Alma-Tadema, Meredith, Margaret Oliphant, Mrs Humphry Ward, Irving, Whistler, Leslie Stephen, Froude, Furnivall, and Joachim. SB is not well enough to go to the Abbey.

The last volume of EBB's *Poetical Works* (1889–90) comes out in January 1890.

RB's estate, proved on 19 February 1890, is valued at £16 744.

Pen takes in Wilson (d. 1902) and Romagnoli (d. 1893) in 1890. SB lives with him from April 1891 until her death in 1903. The strain in Pen and Fannie's marriage becomes evident; they first separate in 1893 and are briefly together for the last time in 1899. Pen has finished the conversion of 'Pippa's Tower' by the spring of 1892 and lives from now on mainly in Asolo. He also buys Casa Guidi in 1893, having sold 29 De Vere Gardens; the Rezzonico is sold in 1906. In 1899 he is persuaded by George Smith to allow publication of his parents' 'Courtship Correspondence', to the anger of a number of Barretts. Pen dies in Asolo on 8 July 1912.

Sources

LETTERS

The Brownings' Correspondence, ed. Philip Kelley, Ronald Hudson, and Scott Lewis, Winfield, Kansas, 1984 – (13 vols so far) is much the most comprehensive collection to date. Most of the material to be covered in the remaining volumes is listed in *The Brownings' Correspondence: a Checklist*, ed. Philip Kelley and Ronald Hudson, Arkansas City and New York, 1978. (Dates of letters in earlier editions should be checked against this usually more accurate list.) See also the usefully annotated *The Letters of Robert Browning and Elizabeth Barrett Barrett, 1845–1846*, ed. Elvan Kintner, 2 vols, Cambridge, Mass., 1969.

For the period after September 1846 it is still necessary to consult a number of other volumes, some of which will remain useful adjuncts to the larger *Correspondence* enterprise:

The Letters of Elizabeth Barrett Browning, ed. F.G. Kenyon, 2 vols, London and New York, 1897

The Letters of Elizabeth Barrett Browning to Mary Russell Mitford, ed. Meredith B. Raymond and Mary Rose Sullivan, 3 vols, Waco, Texas, 1983

Elizabeth Barrett Browning: Letters to her Sister [Henrietta], *1846–59*, ed. Leonard Huxley, London, 1929

Twenty-Two Unpublished Letters of Elizabeth Barrett Browning and Robert Browning Addressed to Henrietta and Arabella Moulton-Barrett, ed. William Rose Benet, New York, 1935

Elizabeth Barrett Browning's Letters to Mrs David Ogilvy, ed. Peter N. Heydon and Philip Kelley, London, 1974

The Brownings to the Tennysons: Letters from Robert Browning and Elizabeth Barrett Browning to Alfred, Emily, and Hallam Tennyson, 1852–1889, ed. Thomas J. Collins, Waco, Texas, 1971

Browning to his American Friends: Letters Between the Brownings, the Storys, and James Russell Lowell, ed. Gertrude Reese Hudson, London, 1965

Letters of the Brownings to George Barrett, ed. Paul Landis and Ronald E. Freeman, Urbana, 1958

Other important EBB correspondence after 1846 remains unpublished in collections including that at Wellesley College, Massachusetts, which holds letters to Anna Jameson and John Kenyon amongst others, and the Henry W. and Albert A. Berg collection of the New York Public Library, which has many of the letters to Arabel and all those to Sophie Eckley.

215

Letters of Robert Browning Collected by Thomas J. Wise, ed. Thurman L. Hood, London, 1933

New Letters of Robert Browning, ed. William Clyde DeVane and Kenneth L. Knickerbocker, London, 1951

Robert Browning and Julia Wedgwood: a Broken Friendship as Revealed in Their Letters, ed. Richard Curle, London, 1937

Dearest Isa: Robert Browning's Letters to Isabella Blagden, ed. Edward C. McAleer, Austin, Texas, 1951

Browning's Trumpeter: the Correspondence of Robert Browning and Frederick J. Furnivall 1872–1889, ed. W.S. Peterson, Washington DC, 1979

Learned Lady: Letters from Robert Browning to Mrs Thomas FitzGerald, ed. Edward C. McAleer, Cambridge, Mass., 1969

More than Friend: the Letters of Robert Browning to Katharine de Kay Bronson, ed. Michael Meredith, Waco, Texas, and Winfield, Kansas, 1985. (This is a particularly helpful and carefully researched edition.)

BIOGRAPHIES OF THE BROWNINGS

(For autobiographical writing by EBB see the essays in *The Brownings' Correspondence* 1. 347–62 and *Diary by E.B.B.*, ed. Philip Kelley and Ronald Hudson, Athens, Ohio, 1967.)

The biographies I have found most useful are:

Gardner B. Taplin, *The Life of Elizabeth Barrett Browning*, New Haven, 1957. This contains much factual detail, some of it superseded but a great deal not.

Margaret Forster, *Elizabeth Barrett Browning: a Biography*, London, 1988. Amongst many other interesting features this presents an unusually sympathetic view – as far as that is possible – of EBB's father.

Julia Markus, *Dared and Done: the Marriage of Elizabeth Barrett and Robert Browning*, London, 1995

Daniel Karlin, *The Courtship of Elizabeth Barrett and Robert Browning*, Oxford, 1985

Roy Gridley, *The Brownings and France: a Chronicle and Commentary*, London, 1972

John Maynard, *Browning's Youth*, Cambridge, Mass., 1977

William Irvine and Park Honan, *The Book, the Ring, and the Poet: a Biography of Robert Browning*, London, 1975

Donald Thomas, *Robert Browning: a Life Within Life*, New York, 1982

Clyde de L. Ryals, *The Life of Robert Browning: a Critical Biography*, Cambridge, Mass., and Oxford, 1993

Shorter items include Michael Hancher and Jerrold Moore, '"The Sound of a Voice That is Still": Browning's Edison Cylinder',

Browning Newsletter 4–5 (1970), and Michael Meredith's 'Browning and the Prince of Publishers', *Browning Institute Studies*, 7 (1979), pp. 1–20, on the relationship between RB and his most dedicated and resourceful publisher, George Smith.

THE POEMS

Because RB has had several periods of popularity or critical attention since his death, his work has been much more thoroughly and extensively edited than most of EBB's, which was decidedly out of fashion for much of the twentieth century. There are, however, several editions of *Aurora Leigh*, of which the most useful for the Chronology has been Margaret Reynolds' (Athens, Ohio, 1992). *Casa Guidi Windows* has been edited by Julia Markus (New York, 1977). The standard edition for most of the poems remains Charlotte Porter and Helen A. Clarke, *The Complete Works of Elizabeth Barrett Browning*, New York, 1900.

Much can be learnt about the history and sometimes the dating of EBB's work from Philip Kelley and Betty A. Coley, *The Browning Collections: a Reconstruction with Other Memorabilia*, Waco, Texas, 1984, which also catalogues the Brownings' extensive library and surviving personal effects.

The completed edition of RB which is most helpful is *Robert Browning: the Poems*, ed. John Pettigrew and Thomas J. Collins, Harmondsworth and New York, 1981.

Still in progress are three more important editions:
The Complete Poems of Robert Browning with Variant Readings and Annotations, ed. Roma A. King, Jr., and others, Athens, Ohio, 1969–; *The Poetical Works of Robert Browning*, ed. Ian Jack and others, Oxford, 1984–; *The Poems of Browning*, ed. John Woolford and Daniel Karlin, London, 1991–.

OTHER

Among the more informative of the many other sources are:
The Diaries of William Charles Macready 1833–51, ed. William Toynbee, 2 vols, London, 1912
James A. Davies, *John Forster: a Literary Life*, Leicester, 1983
The Letters of Charles Dickens, ed. Madeline House, Graham Storey, Kathleen Tillotson and others, Oxford, 1965–

George Eliot, *Letters*, ed. Gordon Haight, 9 vols, London, 1954–78

Nathaniel Hawthorne, *The French and Italian Notebooks*, ed. Thomas Woodson, Columbus, 1980

Ronald A Bosco, 'The Brownings and Mrs Kinney : a Record of Their Friendship', *Browning Institute Studies* 4 (1976), pp. 57–124.

Anne Thackeray Ritchie, *Records of Tennyson, Ruskin, and Browning*, New York, 1892. This also includes some material on EBB.

William Allingham, *A Diary*, ed. H. Allingham and D. Radford, London, 1907

William Michael Rossetti, *Some Reminiscences*, London, 1906

Virginia Surtees, *The Ludovisi Goddess: the Life of Louisa Lady Ashburton*, Wilton, 1984

Virginia Surtees, 'Browning's Last Duchess', *London Review of Books* 9 (October 1986), pp. 17–18.

The Diary of Alfred Domett 1872–1885, ed. E.A. Horsman, London, 1953

Eveline M. Forbes, 'A Visit to Balliol in 1879', *The Nineteenth Century* 90 (1921).

Katharine de Kay Bronson, 'Browning in Asolo', *The Century Magazine* (April 1900), pp. 920–31, and 'Browning in Venice', *The Cornhill Magazine* (February 1902), pp. 145–71, both reprinted in Meredith's edition (see above) of the RB/Bronson correspondence.

Hiram Corson, 'A Few Reminiscences of Robert Browning', *Cornell Era* 40 (1908), reprinted in *Browning Institute Studies* 3 (1975), pp. 61–78.

Edmund Gosse, *Personalia: Robert Browning*, London, 1890

R.C. Lehmann, *Memories of Half a Century: a Record of Friendships*, London, 1908

Index